D1394213

Stay Smart!

Smart things to know about... is a complete library of the world's smartest business ideas. **Smart** books put you on the inside track to the knowledge and skills that make the most successful people tick.

Each book brings you right up to speed on a crucial business issue. The subjects that business people tell us they most want to master are:

Smart Things to Know about **Brands & Branding**, JOHN MARIOTTI

Smart Things to Know about **Business Finance**, KEN LANGDON

Smart Things to Know about **Change**, DAVID FIRTH

Smart Things to Know about **Customers**, ROS JAY

Smart Things to Know about **E-Commerce**, MIKE CUNNINGHAM

Smart Things to Know about **Influencing Skills**, NICOLA PHILLIPS

Smart Things to Know about **Knowledge Management**, TOM M. KOULOPOULOS

Smart Things to Know about **Strategy**, RICHARD KOCH

Smart Things to Know about **Teams**, ANNEMARIE CARACCIOLO

You can stay **Smart** by e-mailing us at **capstone_publishing@msn.com**. Let us keep you up to date with new Smart books, Smart updates, a Smart newsletter and Smart seminars and conferences. Get in touch to discuss your needs.

Smart Things to Know about Strategy

CAPSTONE

Smart
THINGS TO KNOW ABOUT
Strategy

RICHARD KOCH

First published 1999 by
Capstone US
Business Books Network
163 Central Avenue
Suite 2
Hopkins Professional Building
Dover
NH 03820
USA

Capstone Publishing Limited
Oxford Centre for Innovation
Mill Street
Oxford OX2 0JX
United Kingdom
http://www.capstone.co.uk

Reprinted 2000

British Library Cataloguing in Publication Data
A CIP catalogue record for this book is available from the British Library

ISBN 1-84112-034-0

Typeset by
Sparks Computer Solutions, Oxford
http://www.sparks.co.uk
Printed and bound by
T.J. International Ltd, Padstow, Cornwall

This book is printed on acid-free paper

Substantial discounts on bulk quantities of Capstone books are available to corporations, professional associations and other organizations. If you are in the USA or Canada, phone the LPC Group for details on (1-800-626-4330) or fax (1-800-243-0138). Everywhere else, phone Capstone Publishing on (+44-1865-798623) or fax (+44-1865-240941).

for my mother
in appreciation of her love and her courage

Contents

Table of commentary on leading strategists

What is Smart?

The *Smart* series is a new way of learning. *Smart* books will improve your understanding and performance in some of the critical areas you face today like *strategy, customers, change, e-commerce, brands, influencing skills, knowledge management, finance, teamworking, partnerships.*

Smart books summarize accumulated wisdom as well as providing original cutting-edge ideas and tools that will take you out of theory and into action.

The widely respected business guru Chris Argyris points out that even the most intelligent individuals can become ineffective in organizations. Why? Because we are so busy working that we fail to learn about ourselves. We stop reflecting on the changes around us. We get sucked into the patterns of behavior that have produced success for us in the past, not realizing that it may no longer be appropriate for us in the fast-approaching future.

There are three ways the *Smart* series helps prevent this happening to you:

- by increasing your self-awareness

- by developing your understanding, attitude and behavior

- by giving you the tools to challenge the status quo that exists in your organization.

Smart people need smart organizations. You could spend a third of your career hopping around in search of the Holy Grail, or you could begin to create your own smart organization around you today.

Finally a reminder that books don't change the world, people do. And although the *Smart* series offers you the brightest wisdom from the best practitioners and thinkers, these books throw the responsibility on you to *apply* what you're learning in your work.

Because the truly smart person knows that reading a book is the start of the process and not the end ...

As Eric Hoffer says, "In times of change, learners inherit the world, while the learned remain beautifully equipped to deal with a world that no longer exists."

David Firth
Smartmaster

Preface and Advertisement

If you want to understand business strategy, you've come to the right place. This book is a distilled summary of everything you always wanted to know about strategy; and of quite a lot that you didn't know you wanted to know but will be glad that you do.

Belief and attitude are essential for learning. So let me tell you now:

- very few people understand business strategy, *but*:

- business strategy is not a difficult subject

- the concepts are great – enjoyable, intuitive, valuable

- you can use the concepts to get ahead in your career, or to get rich

- you'll find this book easy to read, and it's the only book you have to read to understand business strategy (though you'll probably want to read more, if only for enjoyment).

This book is for anyone who wants to understand business strategy – painlessly! Student, young professional, gnarled veteran of business, someone who owns their own business or wants to set one up, absolutely anyone! There are no graphs or figures in the book (though there is one easy equation!). The language is simple. There's very little jargon. There are piles of examples. So, if you're smart enough to read this, you're smart enough to buy right away, huh?

What are you waiting for? I and the publishers guarantee: your money back if not completely satisfied!

By the way, reading the book won't make you rich or famous. But acting on it may well do.

Richard Koch
Estpona, Spain
January 1999

Acknowledgments

Writing a book that summarizes all the best ideas in any field is a wheeze: it's a pretty smart thing to do. As long as you enjoy the subject, it's easier to write than any other type of book; and yet it has more value to the reader than all but the most brilliant original contribution.

So my thanks pre-eminently to those I consider the giants of business strategy: *Bruce Henderson, Michael Porter, Michael Goold, Andrew Campbell, Marcus Alexander, Henry Mintzberg,* and *Gary Hamel.*

My profound thanks also to the others included in this book who have made me think: *Ivan Alexander, Peter Drucker, Charles Handy, Michael de Kare-Silver, Al Ries, Bob Waterman,* and all the other thinkers quoted; and to *Stuart Crainer* for his research.

My thanks also to those who taught me what I know about strategy and how to exploit it: particularly *Dr Sy Tilles, Tom Hout, Roy Barbee,* and *Barry Jones* at the Boston Consulting Group; *Bill Bain, Dr Chris Eyles, John Halpern,* and *Ralph Willard* at Bain & Co.; *Iain Evans, Robin Field, Peter Johnson, Jim Lawrence, Anthony Rice* and *Scott Schlecter* at The LEK Partnership; and *Alex Birch, Charles Coates, Geoff Cullinan, Ian Godden, Michael Jary* and *Chris Outram* at OC&C Strategy Consultants.

I am also grateful various colleagues and associates in the world of private equity and my own businesses, who have given me the chance to prove that the concepts work in practice or proved the same thing by their own example: notably *Mark Allin, Antony Ball, Denis Blais, Damon Buffini, Dr Richard Burton, Niall Caven, Peter Collins, David Collischon, Sir David Cooksey, Thierry Dalais, Robin Field* (again), *Sir Paul Judge, John Murphy, Andre Plisnier, Charles Rolls, Peter Smitham, Nick Sonley, Harry Tee,* and *Mark Tyndall.* Thanks also to my ex-colleagues at Pick 'n' Pay supermarkets in South Africa, especially to *Gareth Ackerman, Raymond Ackerman, Wendy Ackerman, Nicky Bicket, Adrian Naude* and *Sean Summers.*

That must be enough, surely? Well, not quite. I acknowledge with thanks *Mark Allin* (again), *Richard Burton* (again), and *Catherine Meyrick* at Capstone, and some friends whose interest in business strategy ranges from zero to a hundred (on a scale of one to a trillion) but who nonetheless have provided valuable help: *Lee Dempsey, Shaun Ryan* (né *Etherton*), *Nigel Hudson, Declan McKeown, Donna Macmillan, Elizabeth Miller, Vincente Roig-Yrazoz,* and *Patrick Weaver.*

A million thanks.

Richard Koch

1

What is Strategy?

'Whenever you see a successful business, someone once made a coura-geous decision.'

Peter Drucker[1]

What is strategy?

What indeed! The smart observer should be on red alert whenever hear-ing the words 'strategy' or 'strategic'. If not completely meaningless, 'strat-egy' is typically used to dignify a business policy, and roughly translated means 'what we intend to do', or, even worse, 'the carefully crafted phrases our PR people have cobbled together to sound impressive and paper over the cracks in the board's views'.

Smart quotes

'All competitors who persist over time must maintain a unique advantage by differentiation over all others. Managing that differentiation is the essence of long-term business strategy.'

Bruce Henderson[2]

At the same time that 'strategy' has become a devalued word, challenged only in the business buzzword hall of shame by 'empowerment', the need for proper business strategy has become acute. Smart thinking needs to look beyond the dross usually described as strategy, and discover the real nature and value of strategy. Proper strategy is never bland or boring. It is always original, different and brave. Every business earning much higher returns than its peers has a differentiated and better strategy. Yet the trend in contemporary thinking is towards imitation and so-called operational effectiveness or excellence. Few people are inventing contrarian strategies and even fewer showing the audacity to implement them. But these few smart people will be big winners. The intention of this book is to put you in this category.

Smart quotes

'It deals with the most fundamental and basic questions that involve the very existence of the whole organisation and guide the whole company's future.'

Kerry Napuk

OK, but what *is* strategy? There are a zillion competing definitions. Smart strategists need two at their fingertips.

Definition 1: Strategy = Long-Term Decisions and Direction

Let's start by defining strategy as *the pattern of decisions that intentionally or otherwise sets the long term direction of the company and determines its fate.* For 'company' we could equally well substitute 'organization', 'division', 'business unit', or even 'team'. Whatever the entity, its strategy is the decisions that will determine where it ends up – the shape it will take and its success or failure.

Smart thinkers will note two useful features of definition 1. First, it refers to decisions and decision-making, not plans or planning. Decisions can be made with or without plans. And plans can be made with or without decisions. Decisions are what matter. And the key decisions – or non-decisions – may only become apparent with hindsight.

Second, the decisions taken, or the intended strategy, do not necessarily, or even usually, determine what happens to a company. If intentions routinely led to results, the world would be a simpler and less interesting place. Instead we must grapple with the law of unintended consequences and with the collision of our actions with those of others. Between intentions and results lies the reality we cannot control.

Smart quotes

'Objectives are not fate; they are direction. They are not commands; they are commitments. They do not determine the future, they are the means to mobilise the resources and energies of the business for the making of the future.'

Peter Drucker

'It will make for clearer thinking if we reserve the term 'strategy' for actions aimed directly at altering the strength of the enterprise relative to that of its competitors.'

Kenichi Ohmae[4]

This has led some writers to distinguish between 'two types of strategies: planned (or intended) and actual (or realized)' (Jeremy Davis and Timothy Devinney). This can be a useful distinction for the smart manager to bring up from time to time. For example, a firm may say its strategy is to become number one in its industry (the planned strategy), but the realized strategy may be that it remains number three.

Yet if we go by our first definition of strategy, the decision to become number one is not really a strategy. It may be the strategic plan, but the strategy encompasses the *decisions* that lead to the long-term future.

In this case, the crucial decisions might be (a) building a bigger factory than before, but one much smaller than that opened two years later by a competitor, (b) not adding to the original capacity after the competitor's actions, and (c) deciding to stick to a distributor network while a few competitors switch to a direct sales force.

The only strategy that matters is what leads to results, good or bad. Decisions alone can do this. Press announcements, annual reports, beautifully-produced plans, or cute soundbites cannot do this. The strategy is the sum total of the decisions, right or wrong, that determine the future.

Definition 1 tells us what a strategy is. But it doesn't tell us how to derive a strategy that has a good chance of attaining the desired result. For this we need our second definition.

Definition 2: superior strategy = different strategy

For a strategy to stand a chance of above average returns, the decisions taken must be *different* from those being taken by most competitors. Of course, being different does not necessarily mean being better. But being the same does mean not being better. Being different at least allows the possibility of being better. And being intelligently different, being courageous and not stupid, though it does not guarantee success, can tip the odds nicely.

How does the smart strategist pursue 'intelligent difference'? The answer is to find a competitive advantage.

Competitive advantage means that a business is better placed in its power alley than all other competitors. The business has something that makes

Smart quotes

'Competitive strategy is about being different. It means deliberately choosing a different set of activities to deliver a unique mix of value.'

Michael Porter

'The two elements of strategy are Future Intent and Sources of Advantage. Future Intent is the development of a long-term, far-reaching view and the establishment of a commitment to achieving it, choosing particular markets, as the focus of the company's energies.

Future Intent and Advantage must go hand-in-hand. Future intentions should only be established where advantage can be achieved.'

Michael de Kare-Silver[6]

Smart quotes

'Positioning – once the heart of strategy – is rejected as too static for today's dynamic markets and changing technologies. According to the new dogma, rivals can quickly copy any market position, and competitive advantage is, at best, temporary.

'But those beliefs are dangerous half-truths, leading more and more companies down the path of mutually destructive competition.

'Management tools have taken the place of strategy. As managers push to improve on all fronts, they move farther away from viable competitive positions.'

Michael Porter

it better. This could be a better product. Or better service. Or a lower cost. Or the best people in the industry. Or the best brand or reputation. But better always means different.

And for difference to be lasting, it mustn't be easily imitated. If there is to be real competitive advantage, imitation must be costly, or take ages, or both. By the time competitors have caught up, the leader should have moved on to something better again.

Now, there are two things the smart strategist must appreciate about competitive advantage. First, to be really different you have to *do* things really differently. And to do things differently, you must have made courageous decisions that defy conventional wisdom. Sources of competitive advantage do not grow on trees. They have to be created, and there can only be one creator.

Smart things to say about strategy

'An entire generation of denominator managers has been established who can downsize, declutter, delayer and divest.'

Gary Hamel and C.K. Prahalad, perceptive strategy professors

The second smart thing to know about competitive advantage is that *selectivity is key*. Establishing and maintaining competitive advantage ain't easy. Doing it over a wide front is practically impossible. Doing it in a very focused arena is always the best way to start. To be different and better means cherry-picking. Few products, few customers, few activities. Deciding what *not* to do is crucial. This opens the door to doing things differently, more simply, and better, for the chosen few customers.

Smart quotes

'If I see a company that is substituting money for thinking, I short the stock.'

Peter Drucker

Strategy versus operational effectiveness

There are two requirements for higher returns. One is operational effectiveness: how well firms do what they do. The other is superior strategy: what firms do that is different.

Smart quotes

- 'Natural competition is evolutionary.

- 'Strategic competition is revolutionary.

- 'Strategic competition by its very commitments seeks to make a very large change in competitive relationships.

- 'Differences between competitors is the prerequisite for survival. Those differences may not be obvious. But competitors who make their living in exactly the same way in the same place at the same time are highly unlikely to remain in a stable equilibrium. The value of competitive difference becomes a measure of the survival prospects as well as the future prosperity of the different competitor.'

Bruce Henderson in 1980

Japanese companies rarely have strategies

'Japanese manufacturers enjoyed substantial cost and quality advantages for many years.

'But Japanese companies rarely developed distinct strategic positions. Those that did – Sony, Canon, and Sega, for example – were the exception. Most Japanese companies imitate and emulate one another. All rivals offer most or all product varieties, features, and services; they employ all channels and match one another's plant configurations. The dangers of Japanese-style competition are now becoming easier to recognize. As the gap in operational effectiveness [between Japan and the West] narrows, Japanese companies are increasingly caught in a trap of their own making. If they are to escape the mutually destructive battles now ravaging their performance, Japanese companies will have to learn strategy.'

Michael Porter

Sustainable success requires both. During the 1980s, many American executives appeared to believe that operational effectiveness was enough. Then, the central experience for American, and to a lesser degree, European, managers was the devastating challenge from Japan, based largely on superior operational effectiveness.

Japanese products were higher quality and had better features, yet were also lower price and lower cost. By and large, these positions did not derive from differentiated competitive strategies, but from a common industrial base of superior efficiency and productivity.

The open secrets of Total Quality Management (TQM) and continuous improvement, learned from the two great American quality gurus, W. Edwards Deming and Joseph Moses Juran, who both went to Japan in the

'As the marketplace has got tougher so companies have turned inward, reengineering, downsizes, improving processes and efficiencies, reducing costs and time, marvelling at information technology, worrying about internal change. Many have retreated from confronting the marketplace challenges head-on with aggression, investment, commitment and focused resources.

'The building blocks of effective strategy development lie worn and in ruins in many companies. In this environment, strategy is in crisis.'

Michael de Kare-Silver

1950s, had by the 1970s been inculcated in all progressive Japanese factories. In the late 1970s and throughout the 1980s the products from these factories invaded the West and decimated whole sectors, especially in consumer electronics and autos.

The key event of the 1980s was the American catch-up in productivity. Success with tools like just-in-time flexible manufacturing, led to a belief that technique was everything. The 1990s have seen time-based competition, reengineering, downsizing, de-layering and benchmarking. These techniques have undeniably done more good than harm – at least to

Strategy is making trade-offs in competing

'The essence of strategy is in choosing what not to do. Without trade-offs, there would be no need for choice and thus no need for strategy. Any good idea could and would be quickly imitated. Again, performance would once again depend wholly on operational effectiveness.'

Michael Porter

KILLER
QUESTIONS

OK, so you think you've got a strategy? Well let's see if you're right. Tell us:

- What do you do differently from any other player?
- What investments underpin your difference?
- What's your value proposition to customers that they can't get elsewhere?
- What are your key sources of competitive advantage?
- Which are the 20% of your products on which you make 80% of your profits?
- Who are your most profitable customers? At what rate, each year, do they leave you and buy elsewhere? Do you have a plan to raise the retention rate, each year?
- Who is your most serious competitor now and what are his plans? For an equivalent product or service, what are your costs and your competitor's?
- Do you really know, objectively, what your customers think about your most profitable products/services and those of your most serious competitor in those products?
- Who are the two or three possible new or minor competitors who could be eating your lunch in five years?

efficiency. But the obsession with technique as opposed to competitive advantage has often condemned whole industrial sectors to disappointing returns on capital.

As companies have adopted the same best practices, they've become more alike. They've hit competitive stalemate. Everyone's gone for market share. But market share has proved not to have its usual value. Everyone's become more efficient by outsourcing non-core activities, often to the same companies. Everyone's playing the same game. But the game is a war of attrition.

As efficiency rises, so returns decline. More than 100% of the benefits go to customers, because no-one's doing anything different. Bruce Henderson had said long before that companies could earn high returns only if they found separate ecological niches and avoided head-to-head competition. The 1980s cult of operational effectiveness proved him right.

The smart strategist, like Henderson, learns from the Russian biologist Gause, who invented the 'principle of competitive exclusion'.

Gause put two small animals of the same family but different species in a glass jar with limited food. They co-operated and survived. When he put two small animals of the same species in the jar, with the same amount of food, they fought and died. Coexistence is impossible if animals live precisely the same way.

Decent profitability requires firms to differentiate themselves. Thus the pursuit of operational effectiveness, and the neglect of differentiating strategy, has predictable results.

Successful differentiation: Southwest Airlines and Ikea

Smart thinking is differentiated thinking. In a recent article, Michael Porter cites two super examples.

Southwest Airlines doesn't follow the pack. It avoids large airports and long routes. It doesn't feed you. It won't ticket your bags to through destinations. It offers just one class.

It does fly frequently to its chosen cities. It does offer quick, automated ticketing at the gate. And short check-in times. And low fares.

It gears its investment and operating costs accordingly. It owns a standardized fleet of 737s, lowering maintenance costs. It cuts out travel agents by encouraging direct payment.

Bruce Henderson is a smart name to drop. Whereas most celebrities have a fame that far exceeds their lasting impact or accomplishments, the reverse is true of Bruce. His obituary in the *Financial Times* said it all: 'Few people have had as much impact on international business in the second half of the twentieth century as the founder of The Boston Consulting Group.'

Bruce was what the South Africans term 'otherwise', that is, difficult, passionate, contrarian and entirely original. Born on a Tennessee farm in 1915, he was in turns a Bible salesman for his father's publishing company, an engineer, a senior executive at Westinghouse Corporation, a member of President Eisenhower's team to evaluate aid to Germany under the Marshall Plan, and the head of Arthur D. Little's management services unit. In 1963, at the age of 48, he founded what was to become The Boston Consulting Group (BCG).

Bruce changed the way we think about strategy and BCG was both the first pure strategy consultancy and the first ideas-led firm to succeed so dramatically, going from a one-man operation to the global, 3000-person firm it is now.

Bruce appropriated ideas from biology, economics, systems thinking and military strategy to paint, for the first time, the broad outlines of business strategy as we know it today. He did it provocatively, overturning many sacred cows like the value of accounting conventions such as the profit and loss statement and return on capital employed (the latter, he insisted, was not just misleading, but also dangerous). 80% of Bruce's message may be captured in very few words:

- Competitive interaction is at the heart of strategy.
- If you can't be number one or number two in a business, sell or close it.
- Market share has huge and underestimated value; but changing market share may be easy or impossible, depending on the competitor's position and commitment.
- In general, it is both easiest and most rewarding to gain a leadership position when the market is immature and growing very fast – but only

if the initial leader is stupid enough to forfeit his lead.

- Costs depend on accumulated production, so the firm that has the most accumulated production (market share) should have the lowest costs; the best route to reducing costs was to gain market share.
- The objective of business should not be to maximize margins, but to gain market share; initially margins should be negative and then only marginally positive. Firms should provide greater and greater value to customers (in the late 1960s this was a revolutionary concept that upset most businessmen), driving down costs and prices for ever.
- The only reliable measures of business performance are market share growth and cash. Cash is infinitely more important than profit, which is just a promise (often not fulfilled) of cash in the future. Cash management and redeployment is the most important job of the CEO.
- Neither CEOs nor the stock market should be bemused by short term financial results or by return on investment. If American industry continued with these obsessions, it would be bound to lose market share to Japanese firms who were free of them and who were shooting for global market leadership.
- The only way to superior returns is competitive differentiation. You should aim to be quite unlike your competition; you should search out unique ecological niches. Otherwise, if competition approaches perfection, real returns will approach zero or below.
- Politicians should get out the way of business. Regulation can have a devastating and quite unanticipated effect on market mechanisms and wealth creation.
- Industrial culture needs to change from management–labor confrontation to consensus and co-operation, as in Japan. Labor unions must become company unions, work rules will become relics of the past, and firms will become smaller, generally with 500 or fewer employees and work teams of 10–25 people.

Bruce was always ahead of his time. It was only in the last ten years of his life that American industry, seeing the Japanese challenge that Bruce had long since forecast, began to embrace his concepts. As another revolutionary put it, there is 'still so much more to do.'

Tom Peters is a phenomenon – the world's number one business guru if judged by book sales, publicity and earnings. Indeed, Peters virtually invented the idea of the best-selling guru. Peter Drucker, who is the oldest and best business writer, is certainly in a different class when it comes to original ideas and elegant writing. But Tom Peters makes more noise. He has broken down the distinction between show business and non-show business, and between evangelism and business lecturing.

Apart from admiring Peters' pizazz, which brings a welcome bit of color into the still-grey world of business, is there anything that the smart strategist can learn from Peters? After all, isn't this the man who celebrated 43 so-called 'excellent' companies in his first book, *In Search of Excellence* (1982, co-authored with Robert Waterman), nearly all of which were large, conventional, American companies, only to find that within 5 years two thirds of the 'excellent' companies had hit trouble, and one, People Express, had gone bust? Wasn't Peters the guy who then wrote *Thriving on Chaos* (1987), whose first sentence reads, 'There are no excellent companies'? And didn't Peters go on to publish *Liberation Management* (1992), which sounded the death knell of the humungous American technocratic enterprises he celebrated a decade earlier? The 1990s Peters praises small business, unstructured business, virtual business, fleeting business, ideas-led business. The smart executive may well wonder what new gospel Peters will be peddling in the new millennium.

And yet, there is gold in them there Peters hills, even though it takes some mining. Peters' odyssey is not really a story of inconsistency, more a gradual dawning of some ideas whose force is still not even half appreciated. Among these gems, the smart strategist will latch on to the following:

- Most business has become a service business. Yet very few businesses take service at all seriously. Become a service addict.
- Overinvest in people, front line sales, service and distribution. Make these people the company heroes.
- Make innovation a way of life for everyone in the firm. Like Lenin, espouse permanent revolution.

- Realize that the big corporation has had its day. Leave it.
- Realize that middle management are 'cooked geese'. If you're in middle management, leave it; find something useful to do. If you still have middle management, get rid of it.
- Create your own brand, the brand called you. 'If you're really smart, figure out what it takes to create a distinctive role for yourself – you create a message and a strategy to promote the brand called You.' [In this respect, Peters is really saying that the rule Henderson applied to strategy for business – differentiate to survive and succeed – applies equally to individuals.]

It's different. It's more profitable.

Ikea, the furniture retailer, is Porter's other example. Ikea too does things differently. Self-service, not the usual escort of salespeople. Swedish design of low-cost, stylish, modular furniture, not masses of choice from third party suppliers. Self-assembly, not manufacturer construction. Instant availability from adjacent warehouses, not 6–8-week delivery times. Customers do their own pickup and delivery.

Yet Ikea offers extra services that most competitors don't: long opening hours, crèches, kids' play areas. All geared to one type of customer: the young family that wants affordable style.

Like Southwest Airlines, Ikea has pioneered a low-cost system that, for the target customer, is actually more convenient too.

Who makes strategy and who uses it?

Whose job is it to devise strategy, and whose to use it? Here the smart novice needs a quick guided tour of the strategy industry.

In the beginning, it was simple. The CEO was his own strategist. It is as easy to imagine Henry Ford taking advice from a vice president of strategy as it is to envisage Bill Clinton in a monastery. (Incidentally, Henry Ford was a great strategist.)

But this was, of course, before business strategy, as such, was invented.

(Like all new inventions, business strategy simply appropriated and adapted earlier insights. As Chapter Two will show, business strategy, which some date from the 1940s and some from the 1960s, derived partly from theories of biology and evolution – 100 years earlier – partly from economics – 50–175 years earlier – and partly from military strategy, some 2450 years earlier.)

Business strategy arrived a half century ago courtesy of academics like Peter Drucker and consultants like Bruce Henderson. And the academics and consultants have continued to nurture the Strategy Industry ever since, generously providing research, concepts, and operational support, always at ever-rising prices exceeding anything allowed for in their theories.

Business-school professors and strategy consultants both do two things: they invent or synthesize concepts; and they consult, i.e. offer advice to specific organizations, usually at enormous cost. (Business schools, of course, have as their main mission a third role, that of management training, including training in business strategy.) Interestingly, the consultants, especially the Boston Consulting Group, and more recent specialist 'boutiques' like the LEK Partnership and Mitchell Madison, have been at least as fertile as the academics in developing useful tools and ideas.

As the consultants have invaded the professors' turf, the profs have retaliated with very lucrative consulting contracts. Philip Kotler, the marketing expert based at Northwestern's Kellogg School, is said to have a

IS IT SMART TO BECOME A STRATEGY CONSULTANT?

Do you want to become a strategy consultant? A 1998 survey found that a quarter of MBA students wanted to work for McKinsey, the largest and most prestigious strategy consultancy in the world. McKinsey topped the chart, relegating Goldman Sachs, the glamorous and secretive Wall Street partnership to second place. But is it smart to want to work for a strategy consultancy?

Yes and no. I worked as a strategy consultant continuously for 13 years, which is a long stretch in this industry. The positives are clear. There are few jobs that are as well paid and intellectually absorbing. You can get paid as much or more as a lawyer, financier or even as a head-hunter, but the work (my friends tell me) often sucks, being dull and tedious. Strategy consulting also has nice fringe benefits, including glitzy offices, globe-trotting opportunities, colleagues who are mainly young, friendly, smart and good-looking, and endless supplies of free pizza.

But there are downsides too. You'll work 60–80 hours a week. Your weekends and nights will never be inviolate. Your family or partner may give up on you, and, even if they don't, they'll suffer and so, ultimately, will you. You'll never really feel you're on top of everything. Although pleasant, most of your colleagues will be ambitious and insecure, so competition will, in the nicest possible way, be rife. Most firms operate an 'up or out' policy, so you'll be nervously monitoring your progress in the firm from day one. As in any firm, there are politics and sometimes injustices. And, though the work is interesting, many consultants fall into a rut and, through the sheer volume of work, lose their creative edge. The joys of permanent travel pall quickly. And before you know it, the best years of your life have been dedicated to a firm where you've left little imprint, and to clients for whom you are a hidden foot-soldier.

My advice is to do it, do it when you're young, do it quickly, if possible become financially independent, and then get a life.

daily rate of $30,000–50,000. Tom Peters,[7] the ex-McKinsey consultant who reinvented himself as a celebrity guru, whose stock-in-trade is a revivalist tour-de-force that verges on insulting his audience, charges up to $90,000 a day.

Contrasting with these lone stars, the consulting firms typically deploy large teams of interchangeable client fodder. When I was a partner at Bain & Company, it wasn't unusual to have 30–50 consultants on one client. Fees to the leading firms' largest clients may run at tens of millions of dollars annually. Day rates are lower for consultants than for academic stars, but the consultants sell their wares wholesale. The return on sales for a successful consulting firm before 1980 was 10–15%, but now 25–50% is possible. Returns on capital are astronomical.

Since 1965, the strategy consulting industry has grown by 15% per year, so the smart executive shouldn't be too cynical about consultants. Someone must think they offer good value. On the whole consultants do useful work, and where this isn't true it's normally because the client can't or won't make changes.

On the other hand, consultants nearly always sell more work than is needed, and their fee rates are too high. Is this the market at work, or just poor bargaining by clients? Whereas a plumber or car mechanic may try to take you for 20% more than he needs, the strategy consultant, when challenged, may sharpen her pencil and find that with 'redefinition', as much as half of the price can be lopped off. You generally pay what you say you can afford.

Then there are the in-house strategists, often unfortunately called 'planners'.

In the 1970s and early 1980s it was fashionable for large multinational

EIGHT WAYS TO USE STRATEGY CONSULTANTS TO YOUR ADVANTAGE

1. Talk to them extensively, for free, about the issue you want to address. Tease them by dangling a big assignment. Get them to restate the problem or opportunity. Ask them for their hypotheses. (These will usually be 75% right.)
2. Then ask yourself if you need the work, or are willing to take a chance on the likely answer.
3. If you want the issue addressed, see if it can't be done internally, perhaps with limited help from a veteran consultant. Most consulting firms hate these assignments because they are challenging and not lucrative, and the big firms will likely refuse the work. Fear not. Smaller firms or individual consultants who have left the big firms will step into the breach.
4. If you do use a big firm, demand 50% off the price. Tell them you only have that amount in your budget and they'll have to redefine the work to fit the budget.
5. Meet with the consultants regularly and often. Don't wait for them to schedule meetings. Don't demand output, just a chat about their emerging hypotheses. Shape their workplan according to what you really need to find out. Learn quickly from their early findings.
6. Don't make them prove laboriously what they are sure is right, even if they only have fragmentary evidence. Take it as read. Use their time to move onto other key issues.
7. Do what they say. Make your colleagues do the same.
8. Hire the consultant you rate most highly. You'll get far better value having her on your payroll. Understand, though, that it's 2–3 years per project. After that the consultant will become bored and less valuable.

corporations to waste their money by setting up large departments of planners: Siemens and General Electric each had hundreds of the beasts.

Eventually it was realized that planning was not strategy, and that planners usually subtracted more value than they added. However bright and helpful the planner, he was usually an agent of the head office, and tended to take the thinking and decision-making away from where it should mainly reside: at the level of the individual business.

Smart people never forget that the main player in strategy shouldn't be the prof, the consultant, the planner, or even the CEO – the central character should be the operating executive. The line executive alone has the knowledge, accountability and passionate interest in the competitive battle. Smart executives will never allow their bosses, staff strategists, consultants, or anyone else, to usurp their responsibility for developing and implementing their own strategy. Certainly, the smart executive will use help from any and all quarters (especially if internal rules mean that the help is 'free', not charged to your budget). But as your success is determined as much by your strategy as your operating skill, you'd be crazy not to want and pin down the best possible strategy.

Business unit strategy versus corporate strategy

Business unit strategy is the process or result of developing strategy for a single, self-contained business. The business might be an entire firm, small or large, or a separate, largely autonomous part of a firm: a division or profit centre with its own customers, revenues and competitors. The latter is often called a *strategic business unit,* or *SBU.*

With *business unit strategy* it is easy to see what strategy means and how it can be of value. At the level of the individual business, you are talking about specific products and services and customers and competitors. Your ambition is to become or remain different, better, preferred, and more profitable – probably by concentrating on just some customers (the most profitable and loyal, those you can serve best, those to whom you can offer more value at fatter margins than anyone else can). Actually, you almost certainly won't have just one 'business segment', that is, an area with common customers and competitors. You may have five or ten or fifteen, which each need a separate strategy. But these are manageable numbers, a manageable process.

Corporate strategy is the overall strategy of the corporation. What businesses should it be in? What investments should it make? How should it structure and run its businesses? And how can it create value in a way that no other corporation can?

Too often corporate strategy is just an aggregation of business units strategies – in Gary Hamel's telling phrase, 'the difference between business unit strategy and corporate strategy was a stapler'. Creating excellent corporate strategy is actually more difficult than crafting excellent business unit strategy. Yet it is in many ways more important, the ultimate frontier in creating or destroying wealth.

A smart person's guide to the rest of the book

Chapter Two, *The Case Against Strategy*, examines the criticisms, fair and foul, that have been levelled at strategy, the roles of intuition and analysis, and whether strategy is more art or science.

Chapter Three, *Internal Sources of Competitive Advantage*, examines the idea that corporations should do only what they're best at doing, a useful if surprisingly slippery notion. The key piece of jargon here is 'core competence (competencies)'. We also look at issues like vision, mission and 'bumper sticker' strategies that attempt to encapsulate in one phrase what the corporation is about. This chapter applies equally to over-all corporate (centre) strategies and to those of individual business units.

Classical business-unit strategy is the subject of Chapter Four, *Fundamentals of Competitive Advantage*. The simple idea is that for every part of any business, it is possible to describe the extent of competitive advantage or lack of it, and to identify where necessary the sources of competitive advantage by looking at customers and competitors in each specific part of the business.

Chapter Five, *Smart, Simple, Selective*, argues that most businesses are far too complex and that this hands the smart strategist a wonderful opportunity to place bets at false odds. Simple is both beautiful and highly profitable. This chapter also takes in the importance of the chaos concept and the 80/20 Principle, which often prove better guides than conventional rationalist theory to what is really happening in the world.

Chapter Six, *The Joy of Corporate Strategy*, looks at why the theory and practice of overall corporate strategy has proved disappointing and often ended in mind-boggling wealth destruction. The chapter finds that a new methodology is needed – and available! The theories of value destruction and parenting are outlined and their practical value to corporate strategists drawn out. The chapter closes by proposing a new synthesis of ideas that could lead to an exciting new structure for corporate centres and for their businesses.

The Big Picture is the subject of Chapter Seven. In this highly contentious and opinionated essay, I look at what the insights we can gain from the social, psychological, economic and political context of the corporation. I

KILLER QUESTIONS

- When you say 'corporate strategy', what precisely do you mean?
- Do you mean the overall strategy of the corporation, or the strategies of the individual businesses within it, or both?

conclude that something is wrong both with our large managerial corporations and with the way we have allowed our markets to be set up; and that we need to redesign the whole of our corporate and market systems. While it might seem superficially that these concerns are far removed from the world of strategy, I argue that they strike at the heart of wealth creation and that, if only in her own career self-interest, the strategist must take a view on the big picture.

Chapter Eight, *Crescendo: the Strategist in the Corporation*, provides both a summary of the insights in the whole book and also a map of how the smart strategist will use the concepts of strategy to achieve fun, fulfillment and fortune personally.

Notes

1   The world's foremost business guru.

2   (1915–1992), founder of the Boston Consulting Group and the most original writer on strategy: most of his quotes in this book are taken from *Perspectives on Strategy* from the Boston Consulting Group, edited by Carl W. Stern and George Stalk Jr (John Wiley, New York, 1988). This is an excellent compilation of the *Perspectives*, short and provocative essays written between 1968 and 1998, not just by Bruce, but by many other thinkers within BCG.

3   *Gravy Training: Inside the World's Top Business Schools* by Stuart Crainer and Des Dearlove (Capstone, Oxford, 1998) is great fun and indispensable reading for anyone planning to go to business school.

4   *The Mind of the Strategist: The Art of Japanese Business* by Kenichi Ohmae (McGraw-Hill, New York, 1982) has a dated subtitle now

that Japanese business has stalled and that there is a serious question over whether most Japanese corporations have proper competitive strategies. Still, it's a very useful read, especially on the 'key factors for success' in different businesses.

5   Harvard Business School professor, consultant and leading authority on competitive advantage: his quotes in this chapter are taken from his article *What is Strategy?* in the November–December 1996 *Harvard Business Review*. It's brilliant.

6   Leading strategy consultant: the quotes are from his interesting recent book, *Strategy in Crisis: Why Business Urgently Needs a Completely New Approach* (Macmillan, Basingstoke, 1997).

7   (1942–): those interested must read the fascinating *The Tom Peters Phenomenon: Corporate Man to Corporate Skunk* by Stuart Crainer (Capstone, Oxford, 1997, 1999), now available in paperback.

2

The Case Against Strategy

Dilbert: *Can you at least tell me what our company strategy is?*

Pointy-Haired Boss: *No, I don't want you to lose hope.*

Dilbert, by Scott Adams

The smart strategist will learn much from those who say that strategy isn't useful. Sometimes they are right, if by strategy they mean prevalent approaches to developing strategy. 'Strategy' as commonly practised is often of marginal value, and sometimes does real harm, not to competitors, but to the protagonist! Sometimes the naysayers are wrong, because their view of 'strategy' is fallacious or off-center; but this is useful because it draws attention to what 'strategy' should be versus what it often is. Even more useful, to explore the case against strategy illuminates the many different schools of thought about strategy. The smart strategist needs to be aware of these, and can draw insight from each approach.

The case against strategy revolves around several different views:

- that strategy is long-range planning, concerned to predict the future

- that strategy is an empty ritual

- that all good strategy derives from instinct or insight, not theory or analysis

- that strategic advantage is illusory or unsustainable

- that strategic advantage is the result of luck or evolution

- that good strategies can only be recognized, not constructed.

Let's see how far each of these criticisms is justified, and how they can help us understand strategy's rich texture.

Strategy as long-range planning

There is a strong and useful critique of 'strategy-as-planning'. The essential point being made is the futility of future planning. John Lennon commented: 'Life is what happens when you're making other plans.' Scott Adams chips in: 'There are many methods for predicting the future. For example, *nutty methods such as horoscopes, tea leaves, tarot cards or crystal balls*. Or you can put well-researched facts into sophisticated computer models, more commonly referred to as *a complete waste of time*.' Albert Einstein opined: 'I never think of the future. It comes soon enough.' And the movie maker, Samuel Goldwyn, gave this humorous advice: 'Never make forecasts, especially about the future.'

> ### *Strategy as shambles*
>
> 'In recent conversations with senior officers of companies I have heard these sort of comments:
>
> - "What's the point in looking into the future, it's so uncertain"
> - "Here's a copy of our 1998 to 2003 strategy; actually it's pretty meaningless."
> - "Looking more than 3 years out is a complete waste of time."
> - "Our strategy basically takes historic trends and extrapolates them."
> - "I leave all that stuff to my planning group; they've got the MBAs."
>
> As a result, the whole strategy development process in many companies is a shambles.'
>
> *Michael de Kare-Silver*[1]

Goldwyn had a point. Great fun can be had with predictions that went wrong. My favorite prophecies include:

- 'Airplanes are toys of no military value.'[2]

- 'The mission Columbus has proposed is folly ... the Atlantic ocean is infinite and impossible to traverse.'[3]

- 'There is no need for the Patent Office. Everything that could be invented has been invented.'[4]

- 'Who the hell wants to hear actors talk?'[5]

- 'We have reached the limits of what it is possible to achieve with computer technology.'[6]

Smart answers to tough questions

Q: Why pretend we can make our own future when it is clearly out of our hands?

A: If prediction is futile, you need ways to build in extra flexibility, to catch the curls as they come. If long-term plans are useless, good short-terms ones, especially alternative plans, are more valuable than ever.

- 'There is a world market for maybe five computers.'[7]

Yet attacks on long-range planning are not, or should not be, an attack on the value of either short-run plans or of strategy. Planning need not relate to the long-run. And, even more importantly, the smart executive knows that planning is *not* strategy, or even the process by which strategy should be derived.

Smart things to say about strategy

'Strategy is not the conse-quence of planning but the opposite: its starting point.'

Henry Mintzberg[8]

Strategy as ritual

The critique of strategic planning is more powerful when it castigates the typical process by which companies, especially large, diversified companies, derive their strategies.

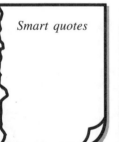

Smart quotes

'In the real world of business, "perfect" strategies are not called for. What counts is not performance in absolute terms but performance relative to competitors. A good business strategy, then, is one by which a company can gain significant ground on its competitors at an acceptable cost to it-self.

'Finding a way of doing this is the real task of the strategist.'

Kenichi Ohmae[9]

In the 1970s and early 1980s, large multi-business American corporations typically had large planning staffs and an annual planning cycle. Each business was obliged to prepare its 'strategy' or 'medium-term plan' for approval by the centre. By 1980 the practice had spread to most progressive European big corporations.

The system rarely worked well:

- It was centralized. The wrong people, those at the centre often took the decisions. On average worse decisions were probably made and the operating managers were certainly demotivated.

- It relied heavily on staff specialists, taking ownership of strategy or concern with the businesses' long term direction away from the front-line operators.

> Smart things
> to say about strategy
>
> 'The only humane thing to do with most strategic planning processes is to kill them off.'
>
> OC&C Strategy Consultants

> Smart things
> to say about strategy

You're in trouble when your company is so committed to strategic planning that it insists on detailed annual plans from each business and when ambitious managers all turn up with glitzy presentations full of multicolored charts, bubbles and arrows.

> Smart quotes

'Strategy doesn't come from a calendar-driven process; it isn't the product of a systematic search for ways of earnings above average profits. Strategy comes from viewing the world in new ways. Strategy starts with an ability to think in new and unconventional ways.'

Gary Hamel[10]

- It worked to an annual timetable, regardless of whether new thinking was required more or less frequently.

- It was ponderous. It couldn't create and implement a new strategy quickly, even if the market or competition required speed of response.

- In practice it was difficult to separate from budgeting: leading to imperfect information being passed upward.

- The flurry of activity – to prepare data, analyses, and presentations – often drove out thought about the few key points.

- It encouraged unrealistic goals that usually didn't take competitors' intentions into account. When the goals were not met, the process became discredited.

- It was poor at following up and measuring whether the plans were being implemented; and it wasn't flexible enough to take intelligent account of new information or changed circumstances.

In 1983, Jack Welch, head of General Electric, abolished his planning apparatus. Since then the annual planning cycle, and large 'planning' or

Smart quotes

'Though plans and strategy are linked, they are not synonymous. A strategy entails at least broadly defined objectives for the firm, and an identified way to attain them. Irrespective of its level of detail, a strategy is, in fact, a plan. Yet it is not necessarily the outcome of a formal planning system. Indeed, the creativity and spontaneity of strategy formulation is difficult to accommodate within a formal planning system.'

Jeremy Davis and Timothy Devinney[11]

'strategy' staffs, have become mercifully rare in the private sector. They are a bad idea. But the smart strategist knows that this does not diminish the need for strategy. Planning staffs and planning cycles were the wrong way to do the right thing.

So what is the right way to do the right thing? It is almost the reverse of the traditional strategic planning approach:

- The right way is to decentralize 'strategy' and pass ownership of it to the management team of each separate business.

- Any staff strategy specialists or consultants should be resources and facilitators for the operating executives, not the prime actors.

- Strategy should only be devised when it is necessary and when there is a clearly felt need for it: when it is clear that the existing strategy isn't working, isn't enough to satisfy people's ambition, or won't work as well in the future.

- Strategy is best developed quickly, using creativity and insight as well as data and analyses. Quantification and analysis are best used to check or refine strategies, not to create them.

- For a strategy to work, it must be simple and easily communicated. Anything that needs to be written down must be back-up to the strategy or a way of measuring how well it is being implemented, rather than being the strategy itself.

- There is no point in tying rewards to the success of the strategy. Either it works and everyone benefits, and it is clear who should be

> *Smart things to say about strategy*
>
> 'Forcing managers to conform to a central planning system is like compelling people to go to church. It stands in the way of true religion.'

most highly rewarded; or it doesn't, in which case there are no rewards over which to squabble.

Strategy: instinct versus analysis; art versus science

When 'strategy' was first applied to management, the laudable attempt was made to elaborate a body of theory that could be applied reliably to almost any business situation. The earliest of these exhaustive attempts was made by H. Igor Ansoff (born 1918), a Russian-American engineer, mathematician, military strategist and operators researcher, whose highly influential *Corporate Strategy* appeared in 1965. It is a step-by-step guide telling anyone with patience, and the ability to follow analytical techniques and checklists, precisely how to derive a corporate strategy: the ultimate 'painting-by-numbers' for strategists. But the real significance of Ansoff's book is that it stakes a claim that strategy is a science, with a robust methodology to follow, and not just an art where one seat-of-the-pants method is as good as another.

Smart quotes

The case for theory and science

'The ideas of economists and political philosophers, both when they are right and when they are wrong, are more powerful than is commonly understood. Indeed, the world is ruled by little else. Practical men, who believe themselves to be quite exempt from any intellectual influences, are usually the slaves of some defunct economist ... it is ideas ... which are dangerous for good or evil.'

John Maynard Keynes[13]

This takes us into a fascinating and fruitful debate: is strategy an art or a science? Let's examine the case for the 'scientists'; the case for the 'artists'; and then reach our own view.

The scientists, from Igor Ansoff to Bruce Henderson to Michael Porter, make the heroic attempt to discover what works well in business, what doesn't, and why. Like all scientists, they want knowledge to be useful. To be sure, they want to chart the world; but they also want to change it. Their work is *prescriptive*: they say how things could be run better. It is impossible to do this without some theoretical framework. Just as medicine can be advanced if we understand how blood flows around the body and why, so business can make better use of resources if we understand which actions are likely to lead to high return on capital and which to end in the bankruptcy court.

Imagine business without any attempt at science or prescriptive strategy. Every possible action by a business person would be a matter of opinion or experience. It would be impossible to state with any authority that one course of action was better than another. There would be no body of theory to guide managers at all, and even case studies would be no more than curiosities.

There would be no point to management training, no justification for business schools, no rotation of business people across narrowly-defined industrial boundaries (for each of these would be a world of its own, with no shared lessons, and the key to success would be to learn from experience within a given industry – there being no better way to make decisions), and (perish the thought!) no demand for business books except as entertainment. There would certainly be no call for management consultancies, except perhaps those specializing by industry.

Smart quotes

'To imply that strategy is all art and no science is to ignore the fact that there is a growing host of evidence that points to specific consistencies in the nature of the way markets and firms evolve and which strategies work and don't work. To ignore this evidence is folly. It is equally fallacious to assume that all aspects of strategy can be boiled down to a neat set of theories.'

Jeremy Davis and Timothy Devinney

Whereas some part of this picture (particularly the absence of business schools and consultants) might have a visceral attraction, a business world without science is almost unimaginable, except as a poorer and more primitive version of the world we know. Progress relies not only on natural selection but also on the diffusion of knowledge about what works well and on the determination of individuals and organizations to use this knowledge to create wealth. If we accept this, the issue is not whether science is desirable but how far we have yet developed a useful scientific framework.

Smart quotes

'In nearly all problem solving there is a universe of alternative choices, most of which must be discarded without more than cursory attention. To do otherwise is to incur costs beyond the value of any solution and defer decision to beyond the time horizon. A frame of reference is needed to screen the intuitive selection of assumptions, relevance of data, methodology, and implicit value judgements. That frame of reference is the *concept*.

'Conceptual thinking is the skeleton or framework on which all the other choices are sorted out. A concept is by its nature an oversimplification. Yet its fundamental relationships are so powerful and important that they will tend to override all except the most extreme exceptions.'

Bruce Henderson[15]

Some people claim that business science is about as well developed today as medical science was in the 17th century. If this were so, we might sensibly forgo any attempt to use theory in business, not on the (silly) grounds that science is not useful, but on the basis that we don't yet have any useful theory. Yet the smart person will recognize that there *is* a useful body of knowledge about business and business strategy – even if the latter has not yet caught up with most sciences, we have advanced beyond the witch-doctor stage.

This book is stuffed full of useful strategic concepts, none of which is an infallible guide to action, but all of which are a great deal more reliable than flipping a coin. The cynic sneers at concepts and searches for exceptions. The smart person applies the concepts to her own business in order to raise its value. In doing so she is only following the example of business strategy consultants, who apply their concepts flexibly, tailoring them (at great expense) to the peculiarities of each client's business, testing with data whether or not a particular concept is useful, and often adding a great deal more value than the cost of the exercise. If business concepts had no value, or alternatively, if they were easy to follow and apply, strategy consulting could not have flourished as it has.

So is strategy all science and no art?

Well, no. For two reasons. One, because business science is *not* as well advanced as most sciences: it's younger, more primitive, and its subject matter is more various and less bounded, involving complex interactions of natural resources, individuals, organizations (groupings of individuals united by a common cause and divided by disparate interests), social and economic rules, competitors and the economic gyrations of planet Earth and its sub-economies. It is doubtful if business science or strategy will ever become fully prescriptive or approach the finality of medical science;

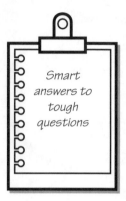

Q: Tom Peters has said, 'there are no answers. Just, at best, a few guesses that might be worth a try.' If you think there are general rules of strategy, what do you know that Tom Peters doesn't?

A: Tom Peters isn't usually this cautious or modest; otherwise how could he think he was making an honest living?

Here are just a few concepts that are generally true, empirically proven and very often ignored at high cost:

- It's better to be a market leader than a follower.
- It's easier to gain or lose leadership when market growth and volatility are high.
- A business which is the market leader in a high growth market has terrific and generally underrated value.
- A business that remains a follower in a high growth market will generally be worth less than thought and may have negative value.
- If there is a market leader with low returns, and at least one competitor with higher returns, the leader can usually improve its profitability dramatically.
- Competitive advantage is always possible, by having lower costs, a better product, and/or better service, for a targeted set of customers. Competitive advantage for any one firm is always higher, or more easily attainable, in certain areas than others.
- Competitive advantage, higher profits and security come from being different. Difference is at the heart of all successful strategies.
- If you want to know the real value of a business, as distinct from its market value, look at its current and likely future cash flows. Profits are fictional. Only cash counts: cash returns on cash invested.
- Successful businesses have a core of profitable customers who have above-average loyalty to the business. Increasing this loyalty is the best way to increase the value of the business.

a sideways glance at economics, a simpler and older discipline than business, should confirm this.

And two, because the *application* of science, however definitive and prescriptive its theory, always involves art, and sometimes art of great value. If that were not true, all heart surgeons would be equally popular and equally paid, and mathematics would long ago have been delegated to mass-produced computers. However high science ascends, great art always applies. *And this is where the 'business as art' school has a great deal to teach smart strategists.*

Smart things to say about strategy (and life)

'Life is the art of drawing sufficient conclusions from insufficient data.'

Samuel Butler[16]

The 'artists' make many related points. Planning tends to be too deterministic, too structured, too unimaginative, too backward-looking, too conformist (to corporate dogma), too data-oriented, too analytical, and too similar (to plans developed by competitors) to be of much help in developing truly created and *differentiated* strategies. To this we may simply say 'amen'.

Henry Mintzberg, the heretical Canadian business professor, advocates 'crafting' rather than planning strategy. He attacks the prominence often given to data-gathering and analysis in the process of developing strategy.

A terrifically useful point made by Mintzberg is that experiments of great strategic importance often occur during the normal course of business

Smart quotes

'Planning by its very nature defines and preserves categories. Creativity, by its very nature, creates categories or re-arranges established ones. This is why strategic planning can neither provide creativity, nor deal with it when it emerges by other means.'

Henry Mintzberg

and without prior thought. But this does not mean that there is no role for conscious strategic intervention. It is precisely by identifying unexpected success as a result of doing things differently – rather than having success by planning to do things differently – that a radical new strategy can be evolved.

Often the successful experiments are 'fledgling strategies in unexpected pockets of the organization'. These can be extended and rolled out on a hugely greater scale; but only if they are noticed and steps taken to replicate them.

For example, the story of how Japanese motorbikes came to decimate the American and British motorcycle industries in the 1960s and 1970s is well known. In retrospect the strategy seems obvious. They started with small bikes, which were the staple of their home market, came to dominate the lower 'cc' power markets, and then gradually pushed up their market share in medium- and then higher-cc segments, forcing the higher cost Western producers into 'segment retreat'.

Except that the strategy seemed far from obvious to the Japanese who were carrying it out! As the head of Honda's US operation in 1960, Mr Kihachiro Kawashima, tells the story, their hopes were initially pinned on

The joy of creating

'Numbers, techniques and analysis are all side matters. What is central to business is the joy of creating.'

Peter Robinson[18]

Smart things to say about strategy

Honda's largest machines, the 250 and 350cc models, on the entirely reasonable grounds that Americans liked large bikes and the less reasonable but more charming grounds that Mr Honda himself had expressed extra confidence in these models, because their handlebars were shaped 'like the eyebrows of the Buddha, which he felt was a strong selling point'.

The problem was that the larger bikes broke down. Honda was therefore reduced to trying to sell their smallest model, the 50cc Supercub motorscooter. This had been imported alongside the larger bikes, but the

Analysis 0, insight 3

Smart quotes

'When you look carefully at [successful Japanese companies, with superb strategies], you discover a paradox. They have no big planning staffs, no elaborate, gold-plated strategic planning processes.

'How do they do it? The answer is easy. They may not have a strategic planning staff, but they do have a strategist of great natural talent: usually the founder or chief executive.

'Insight is the key to the process. Because it is creative, partly intuitive, and often disruptive of the status quo, the resulting plans might not even hold water from the analyst's point of view.'

Kenichi Ohmae

Smart quotes

Intuition rules OK

'Business thinking starts with an intuitive choice of assumptions. Its progress as analysis is intertwined with intuition. The final choice is always intuitive. Were that not true, all problems would be solved by mathematicians.'

Bruce Henderson

Japanese knew it wouldn't sell in America and so had used them as 'pool bikes' to run their own errands around Los Angeles. But when they allowed Americans the opportunity to buy the 50ccs, they did so in droves. Mr Kawashima was astonished: 'When the larger bikes started breaking, we had no choice. We let the 50cc bikes move. And surprisingly, the retailers who wanted to sell them weren't motorcycle dealers, they were sporting goods stores selling to normal everyday Americans', many of whom were new to motorcycling.

Does this deny the value of strategy? Not at all. The strategy emerged; in Mintzberg's language, it was 'crafted'. The successful strategy was different from that initially envisaged. The successful strategy was never written down (until afterwards, by Western observers). But was the strat-

Smart quotes

'Strategy is a system of makeshifts. It is more than a science. It is bringing knowledge to bear on practical life, the further elaboration of an original idea under constantly changing circumstances. It is the art of acting under pressure of the most demanding conditions. That is why general principles, rules derived from them, and systems based on these rules, cannot possibly have any value for strategy.'

Graf von Moltke[19]

egy different? Yes. Was it successful? Yes. Was it based upon definable competitive advantage? Yes. Did it make a difference to customers? Yes. To competitors? Yes. To the industry as a whole? Yes.

A defeat for planning. A victory for experimentation – even though it was not deliberate. But above all, a victory for a differentiated competitive strategy.

Art versus science: a false dichotomy

It is characteristic of the debate about strategy (and perhaps about all emergent knowledge) that opposite positions are taken up and argued shrilly at the same time that both 'opposite' views contain valuable truth. Strategy is art, and strategy is science. The concepts of strategy are useful, but do not amount to a clear blueprint for each business or each time. Data and analysis are valuable, but intuition shows both where to apply analysis and how to apply it. Strategy is not a computer program. But neither is it a futile exercise, or purely a matter of luck. And because it is

Smart quotes

How to combine analysis and intuition

'Define the problem and hypothesize the approach to a solution intuitively before wasting time on data collection and analysis. Do the first analysis lightly. Then and only then redefine the problem more rigorously and reanalyze in depth. (Don't go to the library and read all the books before you know what you want to learn.) Use mixed project research teams composed of some people with finely honed intuitions from experience and others with highly developed analytical skills.'

Bruce Henderson

'Intuition is not a process that operates independently of analysis. It is a fallacy to contrast 'analytic' and 'intuitive' styles of management. Intuition and judgement – at least good judgement – are simply analyses frozen into habit and into the capacity for rapid response through recognition.'

Herbert Simon[20]

both art and science, devising and crafting strategy is intellectually demanding and fun at the same time.

Having dealt with the 'art versus science' issue at length, let's confront rather more quickly the other controversial views of strategy that both challenge and illuminate its value.

Strategic advantage: illusory or temporary?

Since the 1980s, there has been an upsurge in one heresy that appears to strike at the heart of strategy. Consider the following claim recently seen in one company's internal 'strategy' document:

'There is no such thing as sustainable competitive advantage, No advantage lasts for ever. The moment you "discover" something new that gives you competitive advantage, other companies will try to imitate it or improve on it.'

True or false? Michael Porter has do doubt. The trend to deny competitive advantage, he says, is real, but it is a foolish trend luring companies to competitive stalemate.

The death of competitive advantage?

'For almost two decades, managers have been learning to play by a new set of rules. Companies must be flexible to respond rapidly to competitive and market changes. They must benchmark continuously to achieve best practice. They must outsource aggressively to gain efficiencies. And they must nurture a few core competencies in the race to stay ahead of rivals. Positioning – once the heart of strategy – is rejected as too static for today's dynamic markets. According to the new dogma, rivals can quickly copy any market position, and competitive advantage is, at best, temporary. But those beliefs are dangerous half-truths, and they are leading more and more companies down the path of mutually destructive competition.'

Porter argues convincingly, as we saw in Chapter One, that pursuit of 'operational effectiveness' and neglect of strategy is bound to make competing companies more alike, just as at the end of George Orwell's satire *Nineteen Eighty Four,* the animals look from man to pig and from pig to man, and finally can't tell the difference. Result: no-one has competitive advantage and no-one can make above average returns. As Porter implies, ignoring or denying the possibility of competitive advantage can become a self-fulfilling prophecy; yet the pursuit of competitive advantage is as possible and rewarding as ever.

One key corner of the universe where the notion that competitive advantage is dead has made little progress is California. Does Bill Gates, boss of Microsoft and the richest man on the planet, believe that the game is up, and that Microsoft has no sustainable competitive advantage? Nah! (Neither do his competitors, who are forced to conform to Microsoft standards, nor canny investors, who use each pause in the giddy ascent of Microsoft stock to fill their boots with the stuff.) Similarly, everyone knows that Netscape dominates the Internet browser market, and has advantage denied to all other competitors (including Microsoft) in its market.

There are literally thousands of other companies in Silicon Valley that have established and defended competitive advantage in their niches, despite the lightning changes in technology and market conditions. No firm is, or will ever become like, either Microsoft or Netscape, or Cisco, or Oracle, or Ascend, or McAfee, or Security Dynamics. Sure, competitors may clone products, but the leader in each niche is dictating standards and can actually *increase* competitive advantage over time. If this were not true, investors would be making a big mistake with their valuations of the companies mentioned in this paragraph. At the time of writing, the average price/earnings ratio of these companies (the number of times that investors are willing to multiply their earnings to arrive at their value, or put more simply, the number of dollars they will pay for each dollar of earnings) was 53, more than double the average market rating.

Geoffrey Moore, the technology and investment guru, calls companies that dominate their market 'gorillas'. In his brilliant book, *The Gorilla Game*, he describes the battle facing the gorilla, to defend competitive advantage against all comers, and comes to the surprising conclusion that provided they do the right things, 'gorillas' can maintain their status for long periods.

Smart quotes

Gorillas can defend competitive advantage

'At the outset of this race, any mistake by the gorilla could be fatal, and their gorilla status is greatly at risk. But the longer they keep ahead, the more the marketplace forms itself around their standards, the more gorilla advantages they enjoy, the greater the barriers to entry become. Thus their risk decreases over time, and with lots of market room to grow into, their market capitalization continues to expand. These are stocks one does not want to exist from early; they are your long-term holds.'

Geoffrey Moore[21]

But is competitive advantage just a matter of lucky evolution?

The idea that competitive advantage is passé is simply wrong. A more subtle and interesting attack on the value of strategy is the idea that strategic advantage is just the result of luck or evolution. If there is such a thing as competitive advantage, according to this view, it just happens: it can't be planned for or engineered.

Here are some of the proponents of this view:

- The economist, A.A. Alchian, proposed in 1950 'an evolutionary theory of the firm that downgraded managerial strategy and emphasized environmental fit. The most appropriate strategies within a given market emerge as competitive processes flourish, while the weaker performers are irresistibly squeezed out of the ecological niche. Firms are tossed about by unpredictable and uncontrollable market forces.'

- Alchian claimed, 'Among all competitors, those whose particular conditions happened to be most appropriate for testing and adoption will be 'selected' as survivors. The survivors may appear to those having adapted themselves to the environment, whereas the truth may well be that the environment has adopted them.'

- In 1953, Milton Friedman famously argued that 'it hardly matters if managers do not rationally profit-maximize as long as competitive markets ensure that only those who do somehow achieve the profit-maximizing position will survive over the longer term. Markets, not managers, choose the prevailing strategies'

- Similarly, the academic H.E. Aldrich claimed in 1979 that 'environmental fit is more likely to be the result of chance and good fortune, even error, than the outcome of deliberate strategic choice.'

- Finally, the British academic Richard Whittingdon, from whose prize-winning book *What is Strategy – and Does it Matter?*[22] these views are culled, comments: 'the very notion of 'strategy' may be culturally peculiar. The Japanese do not even have a phrase for 'corporate strategy'. 'Strategy' has strong connotations of free will and self-control, but many cultures prefer to interpret events less as the product of deliberate human action, and more as a result of God, fate, luck or history.'

Well, really! One can only say that these academics are in the right jobs. In the real world, and particularly in business, those who don't believe that they can influence events don't get very far!

This is not to deny the role of luck, 'muddling through', and reinvention of history in the description of many successful strategies. Nor are theories of natural selection and evolution to be dismissed lightly. Richard Dawkins' idea of the 'selfish gene' in humans has its clear parallel in the workings of markets to maximize returns. And no less an authority than Bruce Henderson opined that 'Human beings may be the top of the ecological chain, but we are still members of the ecological community. That is why Darwin is probably a better guide to business competition than economists are.'

Yet it is one thing to acknowledge the forces of nature ranged against us, and the apparent cussedness of the universe, and quite another to put up the white flag in response. Even academics should know that there are many examples of successful and quite deliberate strategies, even if all the details were not worked out in advance.

- Did Henry Ford not set out his intent to 'democratize the automobile' in 1909, and did he not know the means – cost reduction through simplification and the assembly line – before he started?

- Did not Forrest Mars Senior set out to dominate the chocolate confectionery and pet food industries by building two superior brands?

- Did Konosuke Matsushita have a vision and purpose when he founded Matsushita Electric in 1918?

- Did Walt Disney simply stumble across the idea of wholesome entertainment and have little part in creating the success of Disney Corporation?

- Did Steve Jobs not have a strategy for Apple to beat IBM in personal computers?

- Is Bill Gates just a brilliant software nerd and Microsoft's dominance of its software markets just an accident? One could go on ...

The only balanced view is that luck sometimes reinforces and sometimes subverts deliberately intended strategy; that strategy should be 'crafted' rather than 'planned'; that intentions must be flexible and respond to what the market is telling us; that unexpected successes are the best guide to rich veins of opportunity; that the environment is never fully controllable, but that it is a good idea to try to control at least the immediate environment; that action may sometimes achieve its intended results, even if the information on which action is based is entirely fallacious; and that crafting strategy is a never-ending process in which market feedback is an essential component.

Henry Mintzberg, 'perhaps the world's premier management thinker' (Tom Peters), is a Canadian professor based at McGill University, Montreal and INSEAD business school in France. An engineer by background, he combines realism and conceptual thought, and is idiosyncratic and often eccentric. I like him because he writes originally and well, and because he is usually right. He is unusual amongst academics in that he understands how companies really work. His first book, *The Nature of Managerial Work* (1973), destroyed the myth that most good managers spent their time devising strategy – or thinking at all! Managers are obsessed with the moment, constantly interrupted, and prefer verbal to written communication. Mintzberg has done more than anyone else (Jack Welch possibly excepted) to drive the stake deep into the heart of strategic planning, and for this the smart strategist is eternally grateful. Mintzberg's demolition job on planning was most useful for highlighting the contrasts between planning and proper strategy creation, which may be summarized as follows:

Planning Strategy	Crafting Strategy
Formalized system	Informal
Calendar-based	Whenever ...
Top-down	Done by all managers
Analysis	Synthesis
Hard data	Soft data
Extrapolates the past	Searches for discontinuities
Conventional, conformist	Divergent, heretical
Detached, cerebral	In the thick of battle
Intellectual	Pragmatic, visionary
Thinkers	Doers
Left-brain, logical	Right brain, creative, intuitive
Dogmatic	Opportunist
Inflexible	Accommodates feedback
One right plan	Experimentation

The best metaphor for strategy, Mintzberg suggests, is not planning but 'crafting'. The craftswoman gets her hands dirty, shaping her clay with mind and body, open to improvisation, adapting the product until it feels right. It is impossible to separate the formation and implementation of strategy; they belong together, comprising one continuous and adaptive process.

The smart strategist will keep this metaphor in mind. The best time to think about strategy is when working with customers and observing competitors close-up.

But can great strategies only be recognized, not constructed?

The final 'objection' to strategy comes from Gary Hamel, the maverick strategy professor. This is his 'dirty secret' (see box below) and partly just repeats the point we have already dealt with about luck. But the smart strategist will also take note of another point: that it is much easier to recognize a great strategy than to make one.

The smart thinker needs to meet the challenges from Gary Hamel and Richard Whittingdon head-on. It *is* a great deal easier to 'oooh' and 'arrgh'

Gary Hamel's dirty secret

'I am a professor of strategy and often times I am ashamed to admit to it because there is a dirty secret: we only know a great strategy when we see one. In business schools we teach them and pin them to the wall. They are specimens. Most of our smart students raise their hands and say, wait a minute, was that luck or foresight? They're partly right. We don't have a theory of strategy creation. There is no foundation beneath the multi-billion strategy industry. Strategy is lucky foresight. It comes from a serendipitous cocktail.'

Gary Hamel[26]

Smart quotes

If you're so smart, why aren't you rich?

'There are thirty-seven books in print with the title *Strategic Management* ... There is little variety, little self-doubt. These texts generally sell at less than £25. There is a certain implausibility about these books. If the secrets of corporate strategy could be acquired for £25, then we would not need to pay our top managers so much. If there was really so much agreement on the fundamentals of corporate strategy, then strategic decisions would not be hard to make.'

Richard Whittingdon

over a great strategy than it is to devise and implement one. And buying a book on strategy, even one as good as the volume you hold in your hands, will not automatically make you a great strategist. You need to be able to read it (if you've got this far, you can probably put a tick against this), understand it (shouldn't be too difficult), and – here comes the tricky part – you need to be in charge of a business, and you need to be able to *do it* with great skill and aplomb. There's no guarantee that reading the book will do this for you. But it may help!

(Another point to ponder is that you don't need to come up with a brilliant strategy to get rich. All you need to do, provided you have some money to start with, is to recognize someone else's brilliant strategy for what it is before other investors do!)

In this respect strategy is really not much different from economics, or physics, or even golf. Reading a great book about economics, physics or golf will not make you a great economist, or physicist, or golfer. But a combination of reading and intelligent practice may make a great deal of difference.

Concluding remarks

The smart executive now knows the major fraternal fights between different school of strategist, together with the barbs thrown at the theory and practice of strategy by academics and others who look from the outside at the money earned by strategists and who can't believe their eyes! OK, it's been a fair fight, and 'strategy' has won on points, though not without conceding more than a few good, well-aimed punches.

Now what? It's time to get to grips in the next two chapters with the heart of strategy, competitive advantage. Chapter Three takes the inside-to-outside perspective, Chapter Four the outside-to-inside view. Both are essential for understanding why and how superior corporate performance can be attained. A rich harvest awaits us.

Notes

1 *Strategy in Crisis* (Macmillan, Basingstoke, 1997).

2 Ferdinand Foch, 1851–1929, French soldier and professor of military strategy.

3 Talevera Commission, 1491.

4 Head of the US Patent Office in the 1890s.

5 H.M. Warner, 1881–1958, denying the need for 'talkies' to replace silent movies.

6 John von Neumann, 1903–57, in 1949.

7 Thomas Watson Jr, 1914–93, founder of IBM.

8 The quotes from this Canadian *enfant terrible* of strategy come from several sources. His two most relevant books are: *Mintzberg on Management: Inside Our Strange World of Organizations* (The Free Press, New York, 1989) and *The Rise and Fall of Strategic Planning* (Prentice Hall, Hemel Hampstead, 1994).

9 *The Mind of the Strategist* (McGraw-Hill, New York, 1982).

10 For the views of this American professor on strategy see G. Hamel and C.K. Prahalad, *Competing for the Future* (Harvard University Press, Cambridge, 1994).

11 Their quotes are from a useful book published in Australia: *The Essence of Corporate Strategy* (Allen & Unwin, St Leonards, 1997).

12 1821–1880.

13 The century's greatest economist, in 1936.

14 1879–1955.

15 In 1977.

16 1835–1902, British author and satirist.

17 American academician and strategist.

18 Author of *Snapshots from Hell*, the exposé of life at Stanford Business School (Nicholas Brealey, London, 1994).

19 Prussian Field Marshal under Bismarck: this quotation is taken from an interesting book about unintended consequences: *The Logic of Failure: Why things go wrong and what we can do to make them right*, by Dietrich Dorner (Henry Holt & Co, New York, 1996).

20 (1916–) scientist and Nobel prize winning economist.

21 His three best-selling technology cult books are all indispensable reading for executives in technology firms and for anyone who wants to understand market dynamics and investment value in high-tech. They have all just been republished, the first two in paperback: *Crossing the Chasm*, *Inside the Tornado*, and *The Gorilla Game* (all Capstone, Oxford, 1998).

22 Senior Lecturer in Marketing and – yes! – Strategic Management, University of Warwick.

23 Board member, ABN-AMRO Bank.

24 1841–1925, French businessman and one of the first management theorists.

25 South African golfer.

26 Well-paid strategy guru.

3

Internal Sources of Competitive Advantage

'Ah, but a man's reach should exceed his grasp,
Or what's a heaven for?'

Robert Browning[1]

The long-distance runner

The heart of competitive advantage is differentiation, and what differentiates one company or business unit from another cannot be built – or rebuilt – overnight.

It is therefore useless to spot a great business opportunity if the team spotting it has no skill in seizing it. In fact, focus on the opportunity, even if it really exists and is a huge pot of gold, will waste resources and lead to losses if the business itself is not adapted to be better than all other businesses at realizing the opportunity.

Therefore the smart strategist will not even begin to look at market opportunities until she has thoroughly pondered what the business is good at. Businesses are like people in this respect. There may be great opportunities for highly-trained brain surgeons in Chicago, but if you are an Italian artist based in Florence, with no skill or interest in either medicine or speaking English, the Chicago 'opportunity' is nothing of the sort.

When I was fourteen, I wanted to be a concert pianist. Why shouldn't I? I had passed all my examinations with distinction and I passionately wanted to do it. Thank God, my piano teacher, without the slightest hesitation, told me to put the thought out of my head. I was moderately competent but nowhere near the skill level required. The competition would drown me.

Many businesses lack the wise piano teacher to tell them what not to do. Consequently they waste millions on enterprises that, however plausible, and however real the market opportunity, are predestined to failure.

Businesses are not simple things and they do not spring to life each Monday morning as clean sheets on which we may write the strategy of the week. Businesses are messy mixtures of things: complicated bundles of physical assets, technical skills, ways of doing things, attitudes to cus-

Smart things
to say about
strategy

'Do not develop plans and then seek capabilities; instead, build capabilities and then encourage the development of plans for exploiting them.'

Professor Robert Hayes[2]

tomers and competitors, inside tracks with regulators or other non-market decision-makers, ambitions and constraints on ambition, characteristic ways of relating internally to each part of the organization, individual and collective leadership styles.

These bundles of things we call businesses cannot erase their past; and any attempt to create a new heaven and a new earth in the business will inevitably cause great pain and is likely to fail regardless. As individuals, we can refashion ourselves in certain areas, but an attempt at complete personality change will lead to breakdown. Businesses too. We can change, but to a large extent we are what we are. In contemplating our direction, we had better start from a realistic assessment of what we are, our distinctive advantages and disadvantages. Otherwise, if we sprint after an opportunity, no matter how much money at our disposal, we will sooner or later be overtaken by someone who is better equipped to win that particular race.

In Chapter Four we will turn to competitive analysis. Before we do so, however, this Chapter looks into something more basic: business introspection and the internal sources of competitive advantage. It is a step that many great analysts have overlooked to their cost.

> *Smart quotes*
>
> 'Among the people who work in strategy, a huge proportion, perhaps 95%, are economists and engineers who share a mechanistic view of strategy. Where are the theologians, the anthropologists, to give broader and fresher insights?'
>
> *Gary Hamel and C. K. Prahalad*[3]

What's the enterprise good at?

In 1955, Philip Selznick coined the phrase 'distinctive competence' to describe what a business is peculiarly suited to do. He applied this to the corporation, to the total organization, but his argument is equally applicable to individual business units. He argued that the enterprise's history results in it having 'special limitations and capabilities', an 'emergent

Philip Selznick gave an example of a master boat-building firm, specializing in high quality craftsmanship whose management decided to expand into mass production of low cost speed boats. It proved impossible to adapt worker attitudes away from their historical commitment to quality and craftsmanship. The new venture failed because the history and culture of the organization did not fit it to the new task.

Selznick observed that a 'distinctive competence' in one area – quality craftsmanship – may amount to a 'distinctive incompetence' in another – low cost mass manufacture. Internal social forces affect an organization's chances of success as much, if not more, than the external market place.

Andrew Campbell and Kathleen Sommers Luchs[4]

institutional pattern that decisively affects the competence of an organization to frame and execute desired policies'.

In the 1990s, the key buzzphrase is 'core competence.' It arose in 1990 in a landmark *Harvard Business Review* article penned by star professors C.K. Prahalad and Gary Hamel. They define core competences as

'... *the collective learning in the organization, especially how to co-ordinate diverse production skills and integrate multiple streams of technology ... unlike physical assets, competencies do not deteriorate as they are applied and shared. They grow.'*

What really are 'core competencies'?

To define core competencies as being just skills or collective learning is too narrow. Really distinctive competencies are resources that one business has and no-one else has. They are either unique, or possessed to a

Take two large American companies in 1980: GTE and NEC. Anyone would have thought GTE much better placed. It was much bigger in sales, cashflow and profits than NEC. GTE's sales were $10 billion, NEC's just under $4 billion. GTE was active in telecommunications, satellites, defence systems and TVs. NEC had a comparable technological base and computer businesses, but was not yet in telecomms.

By 1988, the positions had flip-flopped. NEC's sales of $22 billion played GTE's of $16.5 billion. NEC had become the world leader in semiconductors and contender for leadership in telecomms and computers.

'Why did these two companies, starting with comparable business portfolios, perform so differently? Largely because NEC conceived of itself in terms of 'core competencies' and GTE did not.'

'NEC top management determined that semiconductors would be the company's most important 'core product'. It entered into myriad strategic alliances – over 100 as at 1987 – aimed at building competencies rapidly and at low cost.'

'No such clarity of strategic intent and strategic architecture appeared to exist at GTE.'

Adapted from C.K. Prahalad and Gary Hamel

much greater degree than competition. And resources include accidents of history, physical and mental capabilities, networks of relationships, cultures and ways of working, and many other attributes.

It is usually better to observe core competencies in action and then try to work out their source, rather than the other way round. If an enterprise does something much better or more efficiently than its competitors, it possesses a core competence. What this really comprises can then be conjectured.

'A firm's resources and capabilities include all of the financial, physical, human and organizational assets used by a firm to develop, manufacture, and deliver products or services to its customers.

'Financial resources include the machines, manufacturing facilities, and the buildings the firms use in their operations.

'Human resources include all the experience, knowledge, judgement, risk taking propensity, and wisdom of individuals associated with the firm.

'Organizational resources include the history, relationships, trust, and organizational culture, along with a firm's reporting structure, explicit management control systems, and compensation policies.'

Jay B. Barney

How do you define your core competencies?

Jay Barney raises four questions to ask about the resources and capabilities of your business:

1. The Question of Value

2. The Question of Rareness

3. The Question of Imitability

4. The Question of Organization

On the *Question of Value*, by their works shall ye judge them. Do the competencies *still* add great value to customers? And how, specifically? How is it different from the way that competitors add value? Jay Barney

Caterpillar's chance-related core competence

'As firms evolve, they pick up skills, abilities, and resources that are unique to them, reflecting their particular path through history. These resources and capabilities reflect the unique personalities, experiences and relationships that exist only in a single firm.

'Before the second world war, Caterpillar was one of several medium-sized firms in the heavy construction equipment industry struggling to survive. Just before the outbreak of war, the Department of War concluded that, in order to pursue a global war, they would need one worldwide supplier of heavy construction equipment to build roads, air strips, army bases, and so forth. After a brief competition, Caterpillar was awarded this contract and, with the support of the Allies, was able to develop a worldwide service and support network for heavy construction equipment at very low cost.

'After the war, Caterpillar continued to own and operate this worldwide service and supply network ... to deliver any part, any piece of Cat equipment, to any place in the world, in under two days. By using this valuable capability, Caterpillar became the dominant firm in the industry.'

Jay Barney

quotes the example of Rolex and Timex. 'Rolex emphasizes its quality manufacturing, commitment to excellence, and high status reputation. Timex emphasizes its high volume, low cost manufacturing skills. Rolex exploits its capabilities in responding to demand for very expensive watches. Timex exploits its resources in responding to demands for practical, reliable, low-cost timekeeping.'

Second, the *Question of Rareness*. Resources are only of competitive value if you have them (or more of them) and others don't. Wal-Mart and K-Mart are both discount retailers, but Wal-Mart has grown much faster and then much more profitable because it has a distinctive competence

Culture as a barrier to imitation

'Firms may be at a cost disadvantage in imitating resources and capabilities if these resources are socially complex. Socially complex resources and capabilities – organizational phenomena like reputation, trust, friendship, teamwork and culture – while not patentable, are much more difficult [than physical resources] to imitate.

'Imagine the difficulty of imitating Hewlett Packard's (HP) powerful and enabling culture. One of the most important components of HP's culture is that it supports and encourages teamwork and co-operation across divisional boundaries. HP has used this socially complex capability to enhance the compatibility of its numerous products, including printers, plotters, personal computers, mini-computers, and electronic instruments. By co-operating across these product categories, HP has been able to almost double its market value, without introducing any radical new products or technologies.'

Jay Barney

denied to K-Mart: particular skill in using point of sale data collection to control inventory.

Now K-Mart may be acquiring these skills, which raises the third question: *Imitability.* If a competence is to be a sustainable competitive advantage, it mustn't be easily copied. Sometimes there will be financial barriers, sometimes patents, sometimes a firm may corner the market in the best professionals, sometimes a firm will have a culture that is distinctive and impossible to duplicate.

On his fourth and final *Question of Organization*, Jay Barney points out that 'to fully realize this potential, a firm must be organized to exploit its resources and capabilities'.

Xerox's failure to capitalize on its capabilities

In the 1960s and 1970s, Xerox PARC in Palo Alto, California, was a power-house of technological innovation. It developed the personal computer, the mouse, windows-type software, the laser printer, the paperless office, and ethernet. These could have founded the basis for Xerox to become the most valuable corporation on earth, far more valuable today than even Microsoft.

It was not to be. The scientists and engineers at Xerox PARC were cocooned away from the mainstream corporation and no-one there championed the innovations. Xerox had a highly bureaucratic and myopic new-product development approval procedure. Xerox compensation systems rewarded short-term profitability, which meant maximizing sales of current products.

The case of Xerox is instructive. Core competencies may really exist, and yet be worthless. They are valuable only if they are *seen* as core competencies by top management and exploited as such throughout the organization. In this sense, useful core competencies exist only if they are cherished and properly deployed. The definition of the core competence is a necessary condition for its effectiveness.[5]

How do you decide the core competencies of your enterprise?

It is easier to recognize core competencies from case examples than it is to divine those of your own unit or company. You can read whole books about core competencies and not find out how to define your own.

The concept of core competence or competencies is it-self slippery. It appears impossible to define too pre-cisely. And it's a moving target. An enterprise, like Xerox around 1970, may possess some tremendous potential core competencies, but never recognize or exploit them. Karl Marx said that philosophers had sought to interpret the world, but the point was to change it. So with core competence. It is more important to build it than to find it. Yet you can't build core competencies out of nothing. There has to be a foundation on which to build.

Seven steps to finding the foundation

1. Make a long list of potential core competencies. Consider all skills, resources, physical assets, collective knowledge, culture, expertise, network links, relationships and legacies of history.

2. Discard anything from the long list that is not a plausible contender for a long-term, sustainable source of competitive advantage. For the rest:

3. Ask if the competence is valuable. What evidence is there for this? There has to be a group of customers for whom it is valuable, who will pay good money for the competence. If the competence is not demonstrably valuable, strike it off your list. For the rest:

4. Is the competence rare? If not, it falls at this fence.

5. Even if valuable and rare, can the competence be easily imitated? If so, it won't stay rare for long. Unless it can't be copied, or there are ways of making it very difficult to copy, strike it off the list.

6. Finally, can the enterprise exploit the full competitive potential of the competence? If it can, fine. But even if it can't, don't strike the answer off your list, which by now is probably very short. The answer may be to cherish the competence, and change the organization!

If Xerox had recognized the tremendous competence it had in Xerox PARC in 1970, would it have been impossible to change the organization?

Could a determined new CEO not have done so? Could a determined collective effort from the scientists and engineers at Xerox PARC not have lobbied all the powers within the corporation? Could a brilliant strategist, working in cahoots with the PARCers, not have turned the tide of corporate history?

If the concept of core competence had been prominent at the time, it would not have been impossible. It should certainly not be impossible in a comparable case today. Almost certainly many comparable cases exist today, even if not on the same scale. The smart strategist will be on the lookout for such a case. There may be one lurking in your business today.

7. From the (probably very) short list you have, debate as widely as possible which core competence should form your central thrust for the future.

Decide. Propagate the decision. Work out how to expand the core competence and the impact it has on the world.

And then connect the core competence to something less technical and more emotional. Transcending the core competence, yet building around it, must be something bigger. It's time to talk about this 'something'.

Smart quotes

'Strategy is the organization's 'conception' of how it wishes to deal with its environment for a while. If the organization wishes to have a creative, integrated strategy ... it will rely on one individual to conceptualize its strategy, to synthesize a 'vision' of how the organization will respond to its environment.'

Henry Mintzberg

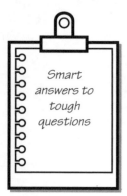

Smart answers to tough questions

Q: Does your enterprise have a clear mission, vision or overall strategy? How do you know? Can you give me a clear set of rules that will tell me whether or not my enterprise has a proper mission or vision?

A: You can't tell by public pronouncements. A company may have a mission statement and no mission. Or it may have no mission statement and yet have a clear mission. Every large company will claim it has a strategy. Few have a clear and appropriate one.

A business knows where it is going strategically if it passes all the following tests:

1. Can you summarize its direction and goal (mission, vision, strategy, strategic intent, or whatever other word you prefer) in one sentence? What is its 'bumper-sticker' strategy?
2. Does the bumper-sticker strategy build on valuable, rare, sustainable and implementable core competence?
3. Does the bumper-sticker strategy give employees and observers a clear sense of 'purpose': why the business exists?
4. Does the bumper-sticker strategy pass the 'competitive advantage' test? This test requires that the business must be or plausibly plan to become better at executing its bumper-sticker strategy than any other business.
5. Does the business have a clear set of values and standards of behavior that underpin the bumper-sticker strategy?

Mission, vision, and strategic intent

Any company or business unit that is going somewhere also has a shared sense of where it is going, and why. The enterprise may call this sense of forward momentum many different things: mission, vision, strategic intent, business concept, mandate, charter, purpose, or even simply strategy. Distinctions can be made between the words, but the smart strategist will usually not bother. What matters is the thing, and its quality, not what it is called.

The 'bumper-sticker' strategy

Every business should be able to summarize its direction, purpose and strategy in one sentence and preferably in a few words. This has nicely been described as the 'bumper sticker' strategy.[6]

Bumper-sticker strategies, core competencies, and differentiation

Bumper sticker strategies are only valid if they satisfy the following requirements:

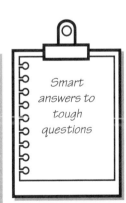

Smart answers to tough questions

> Q: Aren't bumper-sticker strategies just advertising slogans? Don't they demean strategy? What's so special about the strategies and companies quoted above?
> A: No. The great thing about all the companies quoted is that their bumper-sticker strategies are underpinned by distinctive core competencies. Their business systems, too, are all geared to achieve the bumper-sticker strategies. No other firm in the world can claim to be able to deliver each of these bumper-sticker strategies as well as the identified firms.

Bumper-sticker strategies

Company	Bumper Sticker Strategy
3M	Innovation working for you
Apple	Tools for the mind, computers for fun
BMW	The ultimate driving machine
Body Shop	'Green' cosmetics through franchisees
Boston Consulting Group	Breakthrough ideas for business
British Airways	The world's favourite airline
Dell Computers	Cut out the middle-man (direct marketing)
Disney	Wholesome family entertainment, imagination
Domino's Pizza	Home delivery of pizza within 30 minutes
Dupont (since 1900s)	New products for the masses (e.g. nylon)
Egon Zehnder	Ethical, professional head-hunting
Federal Express (Fedex)	Guaranteed overnight delivery
Ford (1909)	Democratize the automobile
GM (from 1920s)	A car for each income group
Hewlett Packard (HP)	Teamwork, sharing technologies for better products
Honda	World's best engines
Ikea	Stylish furniture at low prices for young families
Johnson & Johnson	Serve medical community, super-ethical behavior
L.L. Bean	Treat customers like friends
McDonald's	For the love of hamburgers (fast!)
Marks & Spencer	Raise clothing standards for working people
Mercedes	Best engineered car
Microsoft	Software for human liberation
NEC (since 1960s)	Convergence of computers and telecomms
Pizza Pizza	Two pizzas for the price of one
SAS (Scandinavian Air)	Win customers via moments of truth
Sony	Ingenious, miniaturized new electronic products
Southwest Airlines	Convenient and low cost point-to-point flying
Starbucks	Cult of coffee
Toyota	Become the world's largest car company
Virgin	Debunk the establishment, business as fun
Volvo	Safe, durable cars
Waterstones Booksellers	Great stores, wide range, long hours

1. They must be different from competitors' strategies.

2. They must promise something of value, not to the business, its employees, or owners, but to the world.

3. The core competencies of the business must underpin the strategy.

4. The business must be organized distinctively, to make it peculiarly able to deliver the strategy. And the business must be absolutely committed to doing so.

Commitment: the vital ingredient[7]

A strategy only works if the business is totally committed to it. Most are not.

To be truly committed, a business must have the six attributes below. Assess whether your organization has them:

1. A determination to win in the chosen domain at all costs.

2. A clear definition of the domain. This can be a specific multi-product technology (engines with Honda), a specific product or service (take-home pizza with Domino's), a customer type (Bain & Company, the strategy consulting firm, focuses on the CEOs of large corporations), a combination of product and geographical market (Chess Pizza, specializing in take-home pizza in and around Johannesburg), or a combination of customer and product (furniture for young families with Ikea), or any other clearly defined permutation of technology, product, customer or geography.

Domino's Pizza: The promise of 'guaranteed home delivery within 30 minutes' was made possible by Domino's use of a special envelope to keep the pizza warm, plus a network of motivated delivery personnel. The ability to keep the promise was Domino's core competence. By keeping its lead in the home delivery pizza market, Domino's has been able to build a denser delivery network at lower cost than is available to competitors.

Fedex: When Fred Smith wrote a paper proposing guaranteed overnight delivery of documents, his professor, considering it infeasible, handed down a 'C' grade. And infeasible it was, at the time. What Fred Smith did as CEO of Fedex was to make it a reality: he comments, 'The main difference between us and our competitors is that we have more capacity to track, trace and control items in the system.' This is Fedex's core competence and competitive advantage.

Ford (1909): Henry Ford's outrageous promise to 'democratize the automobile' is probably, and appropriately, the best bumper-sticker strategy of all time. It was a stupid promise, because only rich people could possibly afford cars. But Ford really had vision. His aim was 'to build a motor car for the great multitude. It will be so low in price that no man making a good salary will be unable to own one – and enjoy with his family the blessing of hours of pleasure in God's great open spaces. The horse will disappear from our highways, the automobile will be taken for granted.'

This would have remained a foolish dream but for the core competence that Ford ruthlessly built: low cost, volume, assembly-line manufacture of one standard product, the black Model T.

The strategy could not be imitated, at least not for a generation, because of Ford's greater experience of low-cost production and its greater volumes.

Ikea can deliver stylish furniture at low cost because it makes its customers do all the hard work of choosing, paying for, picking up, delivering and assembling the goods. But in return it offers what its young parents need:

not just great design and low prices, but also extended hours, in-store child car, displays in room-like settings, and instant availability of goods. Ikea's core competence is managing this whole system. There is no comparable competitor of any size.

Honda is passionate about having the world's best small engines. The core competence is technological: to be precise, in multilevel cylinder heads with self-adjusting valves! The product is secondary: just as Richard Dawkins claims that all animals (including humans) are merely throwaway machines for the replication of genes, so for Honda all products they make – whether cars, motorcycles, lawn mowers, or power generation equipment – are just incarnations of their wonderful engines. This stance is unique, and gives Honda a competitive advantage so long as engine superiority confers an edge. Certainly, the world's other lawn-mower makers would be a lot happier if Honda had seen its core competence as making cars and motorbikes!

3. A determination to be the largest in the chosen domain. (Note that this does not necessarily mean the 'market' leader as conventionally defined. The chosen domain may be a small niche. But if there is not a commitment to be the largest in this niche the strategy is fatally flawed.)

4. A deep understanding of the customers in the chosen domain, and a commitment to innovate and constantly to improve the value delivered to them.

5. A commitment to a clear business formula which explains how the business operates within the domain and why it will win over competitors.

6. A willingness to change the business formula if a serious competitive threat emerges within the chosen domain. The commitment must be to the domain and not to the current business shape.

'Every enterprise needs a concept of its industry. There is a logical way of doing business in accordance with the facts and circumstances of an industry, if you can figure it out. If there are different concepts among the enterprises involved, these concepts are likely to express competitive forces in their most vigorous and most decisive forms.'

Alfred Sloan[8]

Is resource-based strategy biased against business unit strategy?

The smart strategist should be aware of a controversy that rages between the extreme advocates of the 'resource-based strategy' discussed in this chapter, and the extreme advocates of classical competition theory to be examined in the next chapter.

The debate is about the nature of competition. At what level does competition really occur: between whole corporations? Or between business units within corporations? If the former, then we can dispense with business unit strategy (in fact, you won't need to read Chapters Four and Five). If the latter, then corporate strategy, the subject of Chapter Six, becomes simply the aggregation of business unit strategies.

In the blue corner, we have the classical advocates of competitive, microeconomic analysis, best represented by Michael Porter, the Harvard professor who plays golf with President Clinton (Porter nearly became a golf pro) and whose 1980 book, *Competitive Strategy*, states quite categorically:

'Corporations don't compete, business units do.'

Smart examples of strategy

Microsoft's U-turn on the Internet

For an example of commitment to win in the domain rather than a commitment to the firm's own way of doing business, there are few better stories than that of Microsoft in 1995.

Astonishingly, the brilliant Bill Gates, head of Microsoft, the software company that had become the most valuable corporation on the planet, initially missed the significance of the Internet revolution. The Internet and Microsoft had bypassed each other, and new competitors – Netscape, Sun Microsystems, and Yahoo! were the most prominent – were well ahead in Web applications.

Microsoft had become centered on its current configuration of the business, and on Windows specifically, and not on defending the domain. But when the danger was apparent, Bill Gates executed a superb U-turn as described in verse two of the Microsoft battle hymn:

> *Our competitors were laughing, said our network was a fake*
> *Saw the Internet economy as simply theirs to take*
> *They'll regret that fateful day*
> *The sleeping giant did awake*
> *We embrace and we extend!*

Microsoft raised its R&D spend by half a billion dollars, entered a whole series of alliances with adjacent corporations that provided services related to the Web, and acquired four embryonic firms with Web expertise. As I write, Microsoft is under anti-trust investigation for its alleged dominance of the software market, including the Internet. Yet only its commitment to ends and flexibility on means saved Microsoft from going the way of IBM a decade earlier.

And in the red corner, we find those who take resource-based theory to its logical conclusion. Michel Robert, head of a large consulting firm, in his stimulating 1993 book, *Strategy Pure and Simple*, is quite robust in refuting Porter's view:

'*Nothing could be further from the truth ... it is companies that compete and not business units. In fact, what will determine a business unit's ability to compete is determined even before that business unit is formed.*'

'*Successful companies are those that can leverage their unique set of capabilities (driving forces and areas of excellence) across the largest number of products and markets. Companies that can spread the heartbeat of their business ... across as many business units as possible ... will assist them in ... prospering ... Business units that cannot use key corporate capabilities are often 'orphaned' from the thrust of the corporation and will have difficulty making on their own.*'

'*Examples abound. Unfortunately, most are from Japan ...*'

Michel Robert quotes several Japanese companies and a few American ones as examples where a core competence or key area of expertise has many product applications (and is therefore deployed in many different business units).

Michel Robert's proposition is that these companies have gained competitive advantage by leveraging their core competencies across many products and markets. This is held to be not just one possible model, but a superior one, which should, by inference, be extended to business generally. Taken to its logical conclusion, business unit strategy becomes simply a matter of implementing the overall corporate strategy, of finding and exploiting the core competencies of the corporation.

Smart examples of core competence-based strategy

Company	Key expertise	Product applications
Canon	Optics and lens grinding	Photo-lithography; cameras; copiers
Casio	Semiconductors and digital displays	Calculators; TV screens; watches; musical instruments
Citizen	Liquid crystal displays	Floppy disk drives; laptop display screens; TVs; video camera viewfinders
Honda	Multilevel cylinder heads with self-adjusting valves	Motorcycles; cars; lawnmowers; power generation equipment
Sharp	Optoelectronics	Calculators; LCDs; compact disc lasers; electroluminsecent computer screens; photosensitive films; optical disk filing systems
3M	Polymer chemistry	*Coatings:* CDs; floppy disks; video tapes; overhead transparencies *Adhesives:* Post-It notes; masking tape; electrical tape; sandpaper
Hewlett Packard (HP)	Instrumentation technology	A large range from oscilloscopes to cardiac analyzers
Northern Telecom Switches	Digital switch technology	PBXs; hybrid analog–digital switches; fully configured offices

Source: adapted from Michel Robert, *Strategy Pure and Simple*

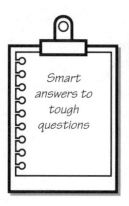

Q: Should the smart corporation have one core competence for all activities or a different core competence for each business unit?

A: Good question. It depends.

If the core competence is the most important key factor for success in each business unit, then one core competence is enough for the whole corporation.

If not, each business unit must have its own core competence (possibly shared with one or more other business units) that constitutes a key success factor in its market.

If the core competences and key success factors are very different across different business units, this may be an important clue to something else. Maybe the corporation should split itself up into two or more new corporations, so that within each new corporation there is homogeneity of the core competence and key success factors.

What's the smart view on the controversy?

Both sides know one side of the truth. The companies cited by Michel Robert have generally been very successful, and probably a major reason is the top-down resource-based approach. Also, it is quite true that many corporations compete principally against one or more 'total' competitors, that is, they compete against the same competitor in a majority of their business. Coca-Cola competes against PepsiCo, Komatsu against Caterpillar, Apple against Compaq, the Boston Consulting Group against McKinsey and Bain & Co, Nike against Reebok and Adidas, Wal-Mart against K-Mart, Exxon against Shell, and, in the UK supermarket business, Tesco competes against Sainsbury, Asda and Safeway.

And yet, on the narrow question of competition, Michael Porter is usually right. It *is* generally business units that compete, and not corporations. To take the example of Honda, its main competitor in motorcycles is Yamaha, which does not compete in cars, where the competitors are

Toyota, General Motors, Ford and other car-makers, who don't make motorcycles. There are other competitors in Honda's lawn mower business and in its power generation equipment. Honda may have a competitive advantage in each of these different markets from its expertise in engines, but Honda pays great attention to countering each of its major competitors. The rules of the game in each market are different, because the competitors are different. The strategy therefore needs to be different for each business unit, and often for many different segments within the business unit.

There is also powerful evidence that business tends to be most successful when it is most 'focused' on one main market and when the corporation is only engaged in one line of business. This evidence is difficult to reconcile with the extreme resource-based view that corporations should be conglomerates based around one very versatile core competence.

Versatility is not a necessary requirement of core competence. The opposite can be plausibly argued. Core competencies are often most powerful when confined to one very specific skill and market and then rolled out globally, as with Coca-Cola, Federal Express and McDonald's.

Nor is it true that the idea of core competencies is relevant only to whole corporations and not to business units. When PepsiCo owned the KFC, Taco Bell and Pizza Hut fast food restaurants, the core competency in restaurants was very different from that in the cola business. In fact the *difference in core competency* is a good reason why colas and restaurants should not sit in the same corporation.

In a nutshell, every corporation and every business unit has its own unique mix of resources and history, and needs to be clear about its internal sources of competitive advantage. To pretend otherwise is to undervalue both resource-based theory and also the importance of competition at

Gary Hamel is one of the most original, provocative, democratic and fast-moving professors of strategy on the planet. A former hospital administrator, he is an American based in California who combines running an international strategy consulting firm with a visiting professorship at London Business School. Together with the cerebral and creative Indian professor, C.K. Prahalad, Hamel wrote the landmark *Harvard Business Review* article, 'Competing With Core Competencies' and the 1994 best-selling book, *Competing for the Future*.

Apart from being the world's most effective elaborator and communicator of the resource-based theory discussed in this chapter – and hence the proponent of companies seizing what he calls 'opportunity share' rather than narrowly-defined market share – Hamel has vividly stressed the creative nature of strategy, and the value of passion, imagination and emotion in the process of 'strategizing'.

He has little time for simplistic formulae. 'We have an extraordinary appetite for simplicity', he says. 'We like to believe that we can break strategy down to Five Forces or Seven Ss. But you can't. Strategy is extraordinarily emotional and demanding.'

Hamel believes that vitality come from difference, and that companies can tap into internal wells of creativity. He is critical of the view that strategy is a job just for the CEO or an isolated, ivory-tower pursuit. He advises widespread consultation and listening: 'Go to any company and ask when was the last time someone in their twenties spent time with the board teaching them something they didn't know. For many it is inconceivable, yet companies will pay millions of dollars for the opinions of McKinsey's bright 29-year-old. What about their own 29-year-olds?' The hierarchy, he adds, should not be one of experience, but of the really valuable resource in strategizing: imagination.

Hamel is also a searing critic of short-term profit maximization and the 1990s downsizing movement, which he and C.K. Prahalad have dubbed 'corporate anorexia'. They are right to say 'a company surrenders today's businesses when it gets smaller faster than it gets better. A company surrenders tomorrow's businesses when it gets better without getting different.'

Well put. And reassuring, too, to find the world's best resource theorist stressing differentiation in terms that might equally well have come from Michael Porter, the guru of competitive positioning. Properly seen, resource and core competency theory is just the other side of the coin from classical competitive analysis. Both are essential and both require imagination and creativity from many different directions and disciplines.

and below the business unit level. Competitive advantage cannot be viewed just from the internal side, without regard to the nature of customers, competitors and the industry environment. It is to this fascinating, ever-changing external picture that we turn in the next chapter.

Notes

1   1812–89, British poet.

2   American professor of manufacturing and strategy.

3   The most important source for this chapter and an introduction to the core competence concept is Prahalad and Hamel's ground-breaking article, 'The Core Competence of the Corporation', which appeared in the May–June 1990 edition of the *Harvard Business Review*. Other quotes are taken from their superb book, *Competing for the Future* (Harvard University Press, Cambridge, 1994). Also well worth reviewing is their *HBR* article, 'Strategic Intent', May–June 1989.

4   I have quoted liberally from the best reader on the subject, *Core Competency-Based Strategy*, Andrew Campbell & Kathleen Sommers Luchs (International Thomson Business Press, London, 1997). This very useful compilation contains the splendid article by Jay B. Barney, 'Looking Inside for Competitive Advantage', from which I have taken all Barney's quotes.

5   The box, *Xerox's Failure to Capitalize on its Capabilities*, is based upon Jay Barney's insights in the article quoted above, although I have added my own spin on the story.

6   The idea of the 'bumper sticker strategy' and all the quotes from Michel Roberts come from his punchy book, *Strategy Pure and Simple: How Winning CEOs Outthink Their Competition* (McGraw Hill, New York, 1993). There is now a follow-up book: *Strategy Pure and Simple II: How Winning Companies Dominate Their Competitors* (McGraw Hill, New York, 1997).

7   The section on *Commitment* has been heavily influenced by Michael de Kare-Silver's very good book, *Strategy in Crisis* (Macmillan, Basingstoke, 1997). The story of Microsoft's U-turn on the Internet is partly derived from this source, which tells the story well and quotes the Microsoft battle hymn.

8   General Motors' boss in the first half of this century.

4
Fundamentals of Competitive Advantage

'Competitors who prosper will have unique advantages over any and all other competitors in specific combinations of time, place, products and customers.'

Bruce Henderson[1]

Competitive advantage is alive and well!

Now, hear this! It's quite possible, in fact very easy, to describe how your company is doing, where it has competitive advantage and disadvantage, and what you can do to increase the advantages and mitigate the disadvantages. Actually *doing* it may not be so easy. But the job of the strategist is first to find out what should be done. And this is not difficult. This chapter will tell you how. Then you'll know more about practical strategy than 99% of your peers. Is this smart or is this smart?!

But first, you have to forget about everything you've been told (outside this book) about strategy. You probably think it's difficult. You may imagine that you have to hire expensive consultants to guide you or devise strategy for you. You may believe that the rules of the game have changed and that finding good strategies is more difficult that it used to be. You may have stumbled across academic controversies on strategy that confuse the hell out of you. You may have a mental block about strategy, the same way I do about anything that involves a modicum of mechanical, electrical or electronic expertise (I can't even use a remote control, and mice of the computer variety really frighten me). But forget all these constraints, inhibitions and beliefs! Strategy is not difficult! *You are about to learn the fundamentals of competitive strategy and if you have not learned them by the end of this chapter, to your satisfaction, send the book back to Capstone and we'll refund your money. No quibbles. Guaranteed.*

Business is a competitive system

Any business or part of a business is a competitive system in which there are only three things that you should think about initially:

- your firm

- your customers

- your competitors.

Within this system, it is possible to describe who has competitive advantage and the extent of the advantage. There are only three possible an-

'Differences between competitors is the prerequisite for survival in natural competition. These differences may not be obvious. But competitors who make their living in exactly the same way in the same place at the same time are highly unlikely to remain in a stable equilibrium. However, any differences may give one competitor or the other an advantage over all others in some part of the common competitive environment. The value of that difference becomes a measure of the survival prospects as well as the future prosperity of that competitor.'

Bruce Henderson

swers to the question, Who has competitive advantage? The answers are: we do (our firm does), a competitor does (or competitors do), and no-one does.

Competitive advantage can only come from two sources: cost or economic advantage; and/or differentiation. Differentiation means that one firm has differentiated its product or service so that an important group of customers prefers that product or service. There are many, many ways to differentiate a product or service – in fact the really fun part of strategy is to invent new ones, and differentiation is constrained only by human ingenuity – but the differentiation works only if customers prefer the offering.

All competition can be described in economic terms. A company that is winning the competitive battle will normally be more profitable than its competitors. If it is not more profitable, that is because the company has made a decision to forego profits today in favor of even greater profits in the future. This is usually a rational choice.

It follows that all competitive advantage can be observed in the simple micro-economic formula:

Profit = [(Price) - (Cost)] × (Volume)

A company that has a competitive advantage will normally be more profitable than its competitors. That superior profitability can derive only from one or more of the following three sources: lower costs, and/or higher prices, and/or higher volumes. Actually, we can simplify further, because higher volumes always mean lower costs (once fixed costs are included in the equation).

Higher volumes are an economic benefit, which effectively translate into wider margins.

For example, a restaurant may have lower prices than its competitors, and apparently equal costs: the restaurant buys its food at the same price as competitors, pays the same hourly rates to waiters, chefs and other staff, pays the same rent and rates and so forth.

You might think that having the same costs and lower prices would mean lower profitability. Yet if the lower prices encourage greater customer traffic, so that the restaurant can turn the tables each day many more times than competitors, the real unit costs for the popular restaurant may be lower than for competitors, and the return on sales and return on capital may be dramatically higher. This is because all the fixed costs (rent, rates, the fixtures and fittings, the cost of the chef and the managers etc.) are spread over a much greater dollar volume of business.

It is impossible for a competitive advantage not to be reflected in the economics of the business. If it is not reflected, it doesn't exist. If it does exist, it means higher actual or future profitability.

This truth has two practical advantages to the smart strategist. One, it means that you can usually spot competitive advantage by finding the most profitable competitor. Two, it means that you can find out whether or not your firm has competitive advantage by looking at your profitability.

If you are more profitable than any competitor, in a particular chunk of business, you have competitive advantage. If you're not, you don't.

Even if you don't know (or can't guess) your competitor's relative profitability, you can discover *your* relative profitability in different chunks of business. You will normally have greater competitive advantage in the most profitable chunks.

> *Smart things to say about strategy*
>
> Competitive advantage matters hugely. It can be gained. It can be cherished and multiplied. It can be squandered. All business is a game to establish and retain competitive advantage.

The only exceptions to this rule are when you are investing in the future by artificially depressing your own profitability (for example, by pricing lower than you could, in order to gain extra volume), or when you are doing the reverse.

The reverse is when you are artificially inflating current profitability at the expense of the future, for example by holding prices so high that you lose volume. In 'strategy-speak' this is called 'harvesting' and means that you are 'selling market share'.

> *Smart things to say about strategy*
>
> Market share is nearly always a valuable asset. Like most assets it can be sold. Selling it is usually a very bad deal.

It follows that you can observe the dynamics of competitive advantage by looking at what is happening to market shares in any closely defined market. If you are gaining market share, it normally means that you are increasing competitive advantage. If you are losing market share, it means that you decreasing your competitive advantage. If market share is not changing, it means that the market is in competitive

The only things that are more valuable than market share are the things that create it. There are only three things that create market share: money, people and ideas. Of these, money is by far the least important.

equilibrium. The latter is rare. Usually someone is gaining and someone is losing.

It is also true that competitive advantage can be inferred, not just from the direction in which market share is going, but also from the absolute level of market share. The leader in any carefully defined market usually has competitive advantage.

A combination of a leadership position, and either gaining or holding market share, usually means competitive advantage and competitive security.

Sometimes market shares flip-flop without warning, but this is rare: the competitive market equivalent of a stock market crash. Usually you can see the danger to market leadership coming, in the form of a competitor who is gaining market share. It is just like observing a car coming closer in your rear view mirror. If it is coming closer fast it may overtake you. Otherwise, it can't.

When you know which chunks of your business you have advantage in, you can do two things about it.

One, you can shift progressively more of your key assets (people, money, physical assets) from the areas of relative disadvantage to the areas of advantage.

Smart quotes

'Perpetual conflict exists along those frontiers where competitive ability is at parity. Very little conflict will exist where clear superiority is visible. The military analogy of a battlefront is useful in visualizing this.'

Bruce Henderson

Two, you can find new ways to reinforce or create competitive advantage. Do this.

What is described above is not quite the whole of strategy, but it is the most important part. Our deliberately simplified view of the world – confining it to your firm, your customers, and your competitors – can and should then be expanded to take account of the wider industrial environment.

Smart quotes

'Business competition inherently has multiple fronts with a different competitor on each front.'

Bruce Henderson

Some industries and parts of industries are more attractive than others. Industry attractiveness can also be described and assessed in simple economic terms.

Sometimes you can change industry attractiveness by your actions: for example, by collaborating with competitors or customers in a new way, or by removing or adding government regulations. Sometimes industry attractiveness must be taken as a given, and the key thing is to concentrate more of your most productive activity in the most attractive markets.

Now we *have* arrived at the whole of strategy. Conceptually, there is nothing more to understand. The rest of this chapter elaborates and give examples. If it does not seem simple yet, it soon will do.

Smart strategists are concerned with competitive advantage, not with competitors

Our real concern is with competitive advantage, which requires consideration of the triad we mentioned earlier – your firm, your customers and your competitors. We are not necessarily very interested in competitors *per se*.

'For any given competitor, there will be different competitors who will provide the constraints for almost every combination of relevant factors. Therefore the frontiers or boundaries of competitive parity will be constantly changing as any one of the competitors changes, adapts, grows, or redeploys.'

Bruce Henderson

If we don't have competitive advantage then we must be interested in competitors, but from the angle of how we can differentiate ourselves from them and how we can find a way of delivering extra value to customers that the competitors can't easily copy.

As Bruce Henderson says, if we're dominant in part of the battlefield (or if a competitor is so dominant, or that part of the field so unattractive that we don't want to dispute the competitor's dominance), we may not actually need to worry too much about competition, except to check that it's not gaining on us.

There is a sterile debate you may encounter about whether strategists should be concerned primarily with customers or with competitors. I mention this so that you can avoid being distracted by the debate should you encounter it. For example, Michael Lanning[3] comments:

'Formulating strategy by identifying value delivery options does not start with competition ... Conventional approaches ask, "What will our competition do?" ... [It is better to ask,] What alternative value propositions will customers have, which we must beat with a superior proposition? Thus organizations should not be concerned with competitors but rather with the customer's competing alternatives.'

'The fewer the number of competitive variables that are critical, the fewer will be the number of competitors. If only one factor is critical, then no more than two or three competitors are likely to co-exist. Only one will survive if the available market shrinks.'

Bruce Henderson

This is half right. You should be concerned with the customer's competing options and with the 'value propositions' (if you can stomach the pretentious phrase).

But you should also be concerned with where competitors are (relative to your firm) in terms of market share, profitability and cost position – and hence your competitive position – and also, if there is a live fight going on, *why* they are where they are and your firm is where it is (the sources of competitive advantage), and what you might be able to do about it.

To consider customers and their choices without considering the competitors who provide those choices is like playing a game of cards blind, not looking at the cards in your hand. It can be done, but it's a reliable way to decrease your cash.

Michel Robert criticizes competitive analysis in these terms:

'The thrust of competitive analysis is ... that corporate strategy starts with an analysis of competitive position. That is a very myopic view of strategy. Furthermore, a strategy developed entirely on competitive analysis will always be, by its very nature, a reactive strategy ...

'Akio Morita, founder of Sony, certainly did not have any competitive data in mind when the decision to introduce the VCR of the Walkman was made. None existed ...

'Competitive analysis is only one *element of strategic analysis.'*

Well, yes and no.

It depends what you include in competitive analysis. If you include, as I do, analysis of competitors, customers, the sources of competitive advantage, and industry attractiveness, and call all this 'competitive advantage analysis', this is pretty much the whole of strategic analysis (not that analysis is the only way to strategize: but that is a different story which we've already been through).

And Mr Robert is quite right about Mr Morita. But the only reason he didn't need to worry about competition was because he was far cleverer than the competition.

If you can invent something that is brilliant and that you know customers will buy and that competitors won't be able to make as well or as cheaply, then you don't need to worry about either competitor or customer analysis.

Most of us are not so talented. If genius was common there would be no need for strategy, except to encourage people to exercise their genius. This again is in line with Bruce Henderson's insight that no conflict exists where clear superiority is visible.

Defining the arena of competition

The first step in assessing competitive advantage is to define the arena or battlefield within which we should do so. This is where most people go wrong. The reason they go wrong is predictable. It's because they look at the total market, not at the right parts of the market. In the military analogy, they survey the whole battlefield instead of carefully inspecting the different theatres of war.

You'll never get to grips with competitive advantage unless you correctly choose the chunks of your business, about which to examine competitive advantage.

In 'stratspeak' this process is called segmentation and the chunks are called segments. Because marketeers talk about segmentation in a rather different (and much less useful) sense, I call these chunks 'competitive segments' or 'business segments'.

Don't be daunted by the jargon. Selecting the chunks of business, the competitive segments, is easy. There are two simple rules:

- If you face a different main competitor in two areas of business (products, customers, channels of distribution, countries, technologies, or any other way of splitting the business that is relevant to you), then those two areas are different competitive segments.

Smart answers to tough questions

Q: Why do you think market share is usually valuable? I can point to hundreds of companies with small market shares and very high profitability.
A: I'm sure you can. And if you care to name any of them, I'll bet that they have a high share of a small market segment.

- Even if you face the same main competitor in the two areas, they are different competitive segments if the market share positions between you and the competitor are significantly different. For example, if you are the market leader in Spain but not in Portugal, Spain and Portugal are different segments. If, in one regional market, Diet Pepsi is three times smaller than Diet Coke, but nearly as big in regular cola, then regular cola and diet cola are different competitive segments.

Now define your important business segments. Most medium-sized businesses have between five and twenty segments.

Assess competitive advantage

In each business segment, find out the extent of your competitive advantage. There are many indicators of competitive advantage, including:

- market (i.e. segment) leadership

- increasing market share

- high profitability (relative to your other segments)

- high profitability (relative to competitors)

- popularity with customers (they rate you more highly than they rate competitors)

- stronger brands than competitors'

- higher quality of goods than competitors (for the same cost)

- higher service levels than competitors (for the same cost)

- any other source of differentiation that is valued by customers

- lower costs and prices than competitors (for the same quality/service)

- higher customer retention (than competitors)

- higher customer retention (than in your other segments)

- ability to attract the best professionals in your market (without paying more).

Usually, the most reliable and objective measures of competitive advantage are relative market share and relative profitability. Market share may be an even better measure than profitability. If you are the segment leader, and not losing market share, you nearly always have competitive advantage. So do you if you are gaining market share, and have a realistic prospect of becoming the leader.

More often than not, segment leadership is correlated with high profitability. You will tend to be more profitable in segments where you are the leader than where you are not. You will also tend to be more profitable than competitors in the same segment if you are the leader.

> *Smart things to say about strategy*
>
> The segment leader usually has competitive advantage. If he hasn't, how come he's the market leader? Are the customers stupid?

Where this is *not* true, you may have mis-defined the segment. Where you have not mis-defined the segment, and you are the leader, and you are not more profitable than competitors, this is usually a great opportunity to raise profitability.

With higher segment share, you *ought* to be more profitable.

The fall and rise of Filofax

In 1990-91 I found out that Filofax, the market leader in paper personal organizers, was about to go bust. This surprised me. Filofax was the market leader. It ought to be highly profitable. Filofax's financial difficulties were an affront to the rules of strategy that I cherished.

What the hell was going on and could I profit from it?

I met David Collischon, the brilliant entrepreneur who had built Filofax into the cult product of the 1980s. He owned 64 per cent of the company and had seen the value of his holding plummet towards vanishing point. Like the press, he thought Filofax's decline was due to the death of the yuppie. He was astonished when I told him that he still had a star business and that the problem wasn't the market, but the competition.

I walked into stationery outlets and found rows of Filofaxes, sitting next to other personal organizers, some branded Microfile and some bearing the names of the retail chains, but made by Microfile. The non-Filofax products looked pretty similar, but sold at half the price. Not surprisingly, Microfile products were gaining market share at an accelerating rate. What looked to Filofax like a market collapse was really a market share collapse. How could they sell them at half Filofax's price, when Filofax couldn't make a profit? Yet inspection of Microfile's accounts showed that it made 10 per cent return on sales.

This might have been the end of the road for Filofax. But I thought otherwise. Filofax was still – just – the market leader, and had significantly higher international sales than Microfile. If Filofax had higher sales than Microfile, surely it should be possible to get to a position of equal unit costs. And Filofax could still command a price premium: not double Microfile's price, but, the retailers said, perhaps 15 percent above. I reasoned simplistically that if Filofax could attain the same cost position as Microfile, and price just 10 per cent above it, Filofax should be able to make 20 per cent return on sales, and also regain market share.

Everyone thought I was crazy. With sales heading south and losses mounting, it was easy to buy a large stake in Filofax and inject new cash into the company. Then came the hard part: the strategy had to be implemented. David Collischon and I agreed to put a partner of mine, Robin Field, into the business to run it and implement the new strategy.

Field cut prices in half and carved out huge swathes of unnecessary cost. Contrary to all received wisdom, the marketing budget was reduced to zero. The wallets and papers were sourced from the Far East at about half the previous cost. The product line was decimated; only high volume lines were retained.

Within two years, product volumes had quadrupled. The share price went from 13 to 80, and, later, to nearly 300. Most importantly, the strategy concepts were vindicated. Even when it was approaching bankruptcy, Filofax was a star business. Market share was valuable.

Filofax did have competitive advantage, even though it was being run very badly. All it took was a determination to attain the cost levels enjoyed by a competitor, and then Filofax took off again.

Unless the whole segment is unattractive (for example, through chronic overcapacity), or unless the competitor is sharing costs with another segment, you ought to have lower costs or higher prices than competitors. This must be true unless there are no fixed costs in the business *and* the reasons why you are the market leader cannot be translated into a price premium.

If it is not true that the leader is more profitable, it is not because it cannot be true. It is because the leader is running the business less well than a competitor who has lower competitive advantage.

Find out how the lower share competitor is running things better than you are. Ten to one it is because he has lower operating costs, not because of any inherent strategic advantage, but because he runs a tighter ship. (In theory, the competitor could instead have greater expertise, but if so, he would probably be the market leader or at least be raising market share hand over fist). If so, you too can run a tight ship too – and boost profits enormously.

When you know where you have competitive advantage ...

Let's assume that you've listed ten segments and assessed your competitive advantage in each. In two segments you have great competitive advantage. You're the segment leader in both and you're still gaining share at competitors' expense. These segments account for only 15 per cent of your sales, but 60 per cent of your total profits. The only problem is that the market is not growing much in either segment.

In three other segments you're not the leader but you are a respectable number two and gaining share. All the signs are that you have *more* competitive advantage than the segment leaders, who have tired brands and mainly complacent executives.

If you continue gaining at this rate you'll be the leader within three years.

Smart quotes

'A strategic sector is one in which you can obtain a competitive advantage and exploit it. Strategic sectors are defined entirely in terms of competitive differences. Market share in the strategic sector, not size of company, is what determines profitability.'

Bruce Henderson

The only problem is that these markets *are* high growth and while this is nice in some ways, it also means that the businesses are gobbling cash like Gadarene goats. Also, in one of the segments, the leading competitor has just had a Management Buy Out (MBO) and is waking up to its loss of market share. In this case, complacency is giving way to aggression. The MBO team has said that it is determined to hang on to its existing 30 per cent market share.

In the other five segments you are neither the leader, nor gaining share. Nor do you have any other significant competitive advantage. Two of these segments are, however, very high growth and they are very popular with stock market analysts. All the companies in these segments are rated highly (they have high price/earnings multiples).

Now what does the smart strategist do? It depends how much of a hurry you, or your boss, is in.

If you have to decide now on the strategy – for example, if a juicy offer for several of the businesses is on the table – you'd have a good chance of being right if in the three high-growth segments where you have competitive advantage, even though you are not the leaders, you do everything in your power to continue gaining share, striving to seize market leadership.

The fact that these are high growth segments makes this even more imperative. If you gain and keep market leadership, the market growth will mean that you'll end up with three huge businesses. If you keep your competitive advantage, these leadership positions will make huge profits.

The fact that the high growth businesses need cash now is good news not bad. It means that your competitors, especially the MBO team, may under-invest. But, being a smart strategist, you won't. You'll get the cash needed from somewhere, even if you have to sell off all the other businesses, borrow money, or raise money from shareholders. You'll make sure that these three segments get all the cash, talent and physical assets that they need.

The low-growth segments where you are the market leader and have competitive advantage are also valuable assets. These too should be given all necessary investment to hold or gain share, even though they are not likely to need much cash.

The other segments, without competitive advantage, should probably be sold. Certainly the two in sexy markets should be, since you'll raise a good price and get more than you give. If you can't sell the segments you should probably harvest them: sell market share by raising prices, and close the businesses if they can't make profits.

'The basic elements of strategic competition are:

- the ability to understand competitive interaction as a complete dynamic system that includes the interaction of competitors, customers, money, people and resources
- the ability to use this understanding to predict the consequences of a given intervention in the system and how that intervention will result in new patterns of stable dynamic equilibrium
- the availability of uncommitted resources that can be dedicated to different uses and purposes in the present even though the dedication is permanent and the benefits will be deferred
- the ability to predict the risk and return with sufficient accuracy and confidence to justify the commitment of such resources
- the willingness to deliberately act to make the commitment.'

Bruce Henderson

If you didn't have the five attractive businesses, you would need to select one or two of the businesses without competitive advantage and find a way of gaining competitive advantage. But the problem is this case is too much opportunity, not too little, so you don't need the challenge of bootstrapping competitive advantage where none exists today.

And what would the smart strategist do if she had more time? Four things. First, she would identify the *source* of competitive advantage in each case. Second, she would work out how to *create* competitive advantage in each case. Third, she would assess segment attractiveness. Finally, she would see if she could influence segment attractiveness.

Identify the source of competitive advantage

It's important to know the source of competitive advantage in order to assess its sustainability and also to make it more sustainable: to build on it, deepen it and add to it.

The source of competitive advantage should be related back to the firm's core competence or competencies as discussed in Chapter Three. Unless competitive advantage in the key priority segments is compatible with the firm's core competence, either the latter should be changed or the priority segments redefined. If neither of these approaches appeals, it is a good indicator that the firm's organizational structure is wrong and a spin-off required (see Chapter Six).

Remember that competitive advantage falls under two main (often complementary) headings: cost or economic advantage; and differentiation. A cost advantage exists when the total system cost for delivering a product or service, including all investment and overhead costs, is lower for one

KILLER
QUESTIONS!

- In this segment, who has lower costs, us or Firm X, our main competitor?
- Firm X has lower prices than us and larger market share. They also seem to like the segment more than we do, which suggests that they have higher profitability.
- If Firm X has lower costs than us, can we copy what they do in order to lower our costs? If not, do we really want to be in a business where we are at a permanent economic disadvantage?

player than for all other competitors. Most executives implicitly assume that competitors have equal costs. Typically, this isn't so.

It's wonderful to enjoy a structural cost advantage, based either on larger scale or doing things differently than competitors.

If the cost advantage is based on scale, then market share must be protected, or else the advantage may be squandered.

If the cost advantage is based on doing things differently, the smart strategist will be on the lookout for any competitor, especially a new one, that appears to have cottoned on to the way we do business. The key to sustaining the cost advantage that is based on differentiation is to sharpen the differences between our approach and the competitors'. Whatever we do differently, do more of it and take it to its logical conclusion. Build on the firm's core competencies of the corporation to deepen the differentiation and the core competencies simultaneously.

Wonderful, wonderful differentiation!

Differentiation is not just a source of cost advantage; it is also the main source of competitive advantage in its own right. And there can be an

Smart quotes

infinite number of sources of differentiation. Being different does not guarantee success. But success nearly always requires differentiation. The key is to find a form of differentiation that satisfies two criteria:

- the differentiation must be liked by a significant group of customers

- the differentiation must not confer a margin disadvantage. Ideally, it should confer a margin advantage.

Finding a margin advantage through popular differentiation is not as difficult as it sounds. Remember the examples of Southwest Airlines and Ikea, where a package of lower costs (e.g. no meals on planes, no delivery of furniture) is combined with other attributes (short check-in times, in-store child care) that

Smart quotes

'All competitors are specialists. No two competitors can serve exactly the same customers, at exactly the same time, in exactly the same way, at exactly the same cost. The differences between competitors are the measure of their specialization.'

Richard K. Lochridge

are valued by the target customers. In aggregate, the costs are lower, yet customer satisfaction higher.

Inventing new twists on the old theme of self-service – delegating some of the tasks to the customers – is still one of the most fruitful sources of differentiation, where low costs can coexist with happier customers, particularly if some of the benefit is passed on in lower prices. The smart strategist always aims to create a virtuous circle, where lower prices lead to higher volumes which lead to still lower prices which lead to still higher volumes ...

Ponder these ways of differentiating, and think whether they could be applied to your business:

KILLER QUESTIONS

Do we have a product or service or delivery system that is sharply different from that of all our competitors? Wouldn't we make much more money if we did?

- extraordinary service: what Michael de Kare-Silver calls 'service hustle'

- emotion, based on branding and what is fashionable or identified with one particular customer group, like young professionals, gays or retired folk

- superior performance (e.g. BMWs)

- safety and durability (e.g. Volvos)

- extra features (e.g. Microsoft's Windows)

- instant or rapid availability (e.g. McDonald's)

- personalization (e.g. Swatch watches available in limited editions)

Smart examples of strategy

- extra services (e.g. a service station that always washes windshields)

- convenience (e.g. Pick 'n' Pay supermarkets in South Africa, where you can pay your utility bills at the checkout)

- unusual speed (e.g. Domino's pizza)

- unusual values (e.g. Body Shop standing up for green values and the dispossessed)

- new channels of distribution (e.g. Amazon.com in bookselling, Dell Computers, telephone banking and insurance services)

- new dimensions of self-service (e.g. Ikea)

> ### *Service hustle as a basis of differentiation*
>
> 'Service is no longer enough. I shall call it Hustle. What is the basis of success for the likes of McDonald's, British Airways, USAA, Nordstrom, Caltex, Ritz Carlton and UPS? It is not just customer service. It is extraordinary hustle. It is going beyond customers' expectations and creating levels of service and standards that had not been imagined.
>
> 'It's about establishing a relationship with your customers that goes beyond the immediate transaction but builds into achieving a life-time commitment from that customer to work together with you to find mutual advantage and satisfaction.'
>
> *Michael de Kare-Silver*[6]

- slicker packaging and presentation (e.g. toothpaste in a dispenser)

- friendliness (e.g. L. L. Bean stores)

- attractive staff (don't you think Virgin stewards and stewardesses are better looking?)

You can often get rich simply by applying to your industry or sub-industry what has worked well in another industry, or another country, or another technology. The real jackpot, however, comes when you invent a completely new source of differentiation. Why not have a go?

Industry and Segment Attractiveness

The final weapon in the smart strategist's arsenal is a tool for assessing and influencing not just competitive advantage, but also industry or segment attractiveness. The pioneering work here comes from Michael Porter.[7]

Michael Porter is clearly very smart. Now Harvard Business School's star professor, he gained tenure at 26, has a degree in aeronautical engineering, plays golf to professional standard, was the founder of Monitor, the excellent strategy consulting firm, and has made countless millions from his books, seminars, and videos. He has also make his mark as economic adviser to Massachusetts, the US congress and several countries. He is probably the best writer on competitive advantage in the world, the late Bruce Henderson only excepted.

Porter's trademark is rigorous economic frameworks, derived in large part from classical economics (with a particular debt to the great Joseph Schumpeter), and lucidly applied to business and nation states. Though his latest work has been concerned with *The Competitive Advantage of Nations* (the title of his 1990 book), his most influential book remains the brilliant *Competitive Strategy* (1980). Porter's most valuable single point in the book is that there were only three generic sources of competitive advantage – lowest cost, differentiation, and focus (niche) strategies. More recently, Porter has tended to collapse 'focus' into differentiation, now talking about 'the two basic forms of competitive advantage: cost leadership and differentiation'. The approach in this chapter has followed Porter's lead.

In *Competitive Strategy*, Porter also created his famous Five [competitive] Forces model. Each industry or business has its attractiveness influenced not just by rivalry amongst existing competitors (the traditional focus of competitive strategy and still, in my opinion, by far the most important single force) but by four other environmental forces:

1. The entry or threat of entry from new competitors. If there are high returns and low barriers to entry, new firms, like frogs, will come, and will depress returns.
2. Substitutes are another threat. Close substitutes will constrain the prices you can realize.
3. The bargaining power of buyers. The balance of power in the industry is crucial. For example, retailers with a strong brand will normally have great power over their individual customers. On the other hand, the balance of

SMART PEOPLE
TO HAVE ON
YOUR SIDE:

MICHAEL
PORTER
(BORN 1947)

> power between manufacturers of fast-moving consumer goods and the manufacturers' buyers – the retailer chains – may tilt either way. If the manufacturers have strong proprietary brands and there are many retailers, the manufacturers may have the balance of power. On the other hand, if the retailers themselves have stronger brands than the manufacturers, and if the retail industry is very concentrated, it may be the latter that has the whip hand. In general, the more concentrated side (buyers or the industry) will have an advantage.
>
> 4. The bargaining power of the suppliers. For retailers, manufacturers are their suppliers. For the manufacturers, it is the suppliers of raw material and subcontractors who are the suppliers. If there are few quality suppliers, they may constrain profitability.

Porter's framework was meant as a way to evaluate the extent of competitive advantage available. But it is now increasingly used, too, to help tilt the field this way.

My personal view is that the framework is more useful in pointing out the forces to be reckoned with than in providing an objective basis for evaluating the forces. Two different teams of assessors, faced with the same data, can come to very different conclusions on the extent of available competitive advantage, depending on how they weight the data and how creatively they can see ways to turn the forces to their advantage. Porter's book contains far more than the five forces model and I feel happier recommending the book than the model.

Another model for assessing industry attractiveness

Porter's five forces do not cover four other factors that can help to describe industry or segment attractiveness:

- Profitability in the industry or segment, as measured by return on capital employed (ROCE). Profitability, it is true, is a result and not a force. But it is a powerful piece of evidence that has already processed many of the data that go into making an industry more or less attractive. For example, even very 'competitive' professional services businesses (like consulting, accounting or software businesses) have very high return on capital, often because they have very little capital. Even measured by return on sales, these professional services are, in aggregate, amazingly profitable. Their attractiveness is understated by models like the Five Forces.

- The trend in ROCE is also a key indicator of future competitive segment profitability and attractiveness.

- The market growth rate is also an indicator of attractiveness.

Don't get stuck in the middle

'The firm failing to develop its strategy in at least one of the three directions [lowest cost, differentiation, or focus] – a firm that is *stuck in the middle* – is in an extremely poor strategic situation. The firm lacks the market share, capital investment, and resolve to play the low-cost game, the industry-wide differentiation necessary to obviate the need for a low-cost position, or the focus to create differentiation or low cost in a more limited sphere.

'The firm stuck in the middle is almost guaranteed low profitability. It either loses the high-volume customers who demand low prices or must bid away its profits to get this business away from low-cost firms. Yet it also loses high-margin business – the cream – to the firms who are focused on high-margin targets or have achieved differentiation overall.'

Michael Porter

- The current balance between total customer demand and available industry capacity is also significant. Some industries (like steel or airlines) may have little danger from new entrants but a huge overhang of capacity, and are correspondingly unattractive.

In *The Financial Times Guide to Strategy,* I lay out an alternative model to Porter's Five Forces for assessing industry attractiveness. Instead of including the extent of competitive rivalry as one of the forces, I assume that competitive advantage has already been computed (as in this chapter), and then go on to score eight factors to arrive at a total score for each industry or segment. Here is a summary:

Industry/segment attractiveness checklist

Factors	Minimum score	Maximum score
Current segment weighted ROCE	0	40
Trend in ROCE	0	10
Barriers to entry of new competitors	0	10
Future market growth rate	0	10
Demand/capacity balance	−20	0
Threat from substituting products, services or technologies	−20	0
Bargaining power of suppliers	0	10
Bargaining power of customers	0	20

The industry/segment attractiveness matrix therefore can score between −40 to +100. In the hands of the same assessors, it is a fairly reliable measure of the relative attractiveness of all the segments in which your firm participates.

Influencing segment and industry attractiveness

Segment or industry attractiveness is not a given. The smart strategist will explore every opportunity to improve it. Each dimension of attractiveness may be susceptible to influence:

Attractiveness factor	Example of how to influence the factor
Industry ROCE/ trend in ROCE	Cost reduction
	Price increases from adding extra value
	Price increases from influencing fellow suppliers
	Working capital reductions from better ranging, more flexible manufacturing, and squeezing suppliers
Barriers to new entrants	Raise barriers by investment or by pre-empting the best sites or bottleneck resources
	Pretend the industry is more competitive or lower profit than it really is
	Lock in key staff
	Give latest new entrant a hard time
Market growth	Stimulate market growth by innovation
Capacity/demand balance	Encourage retirement of excess capacity
	Acquire a competitor and close excess capacity
	Find new use for capacity
	Increase exports
Threat from substitutes	Lower cost of your product/service
	Raise quality above substitutes
	Raise performance/features above substitutes
	Turn substitutes into complements
Bargaining power of suppliers	Develop and encourage new suppliers
	Ally with one supplier and lock in on favorable terms

Attractiveness factor	Example of how to influence the factor
Bargaining power of customers	Shift balance of power by acquiring competitor(s)
	Differentiate so that there is only one source of what you have to offer
	Build brands
	Build customer loyalty through superior delivery and lock-in mechanisms

Conclusion

The smart strategist has now defined his firm's competitive advantage and made it congruent with the firm's core competences – and vice versa. He's identified the priority segments, and is determined to increase competitive advantage in each segment. He knows how. He's also tilting segment attractiveness in his favor. Bravo!

But is he trying to do too much. Is he focused enough? Is his strategy simple enough? Is his company? Has he really latched on to the most powerful levers to achieve what he wants?

All will be revealed in the next episode.

[In my earlier book on strategy, *The Financial Times Guide to Strategy* (FT/Pitman, London, 1995, revised edition 1999) I give a methodical and practical step by step account of how to create a business unit strategy. Any smart executive who wants a more detailed account than I could give in this chapter is recommended to consult it.]

Notes

1   The words of Bruce Henderson, John Clarkeson and Richard Lochridge are all taken from *Perspectives on Strategy from The Boston Consulting Group*, edited by Carl W. Stern and George Stalk, Jr. (John Wiley & Sons, New York, 1998).

2   1856–1950, British dramatist and writer, from his play *Arms and the Man*. For this quotation I am indebted to Eileen C. Shapiro in her very witty book, *The Seven Deadly Sins of Business* (Capstone, Oxford, 1988).

3   To be fair to Michael Lanning, he does deliver much of value in his new book, *Delivering Profitable Value* (Capstone, Oxford, 1998).

4   Boston Consulting Group veteran

5   Barry J. Gibbons, *If You Want to Make God Really Laugh Show Him Your Business Plan* (Capstone, Oxford, 1998).

6   *Strategy in Crisis* (Macmillan, Basingstoke, 1997).

7   The smart strategist should read *Competitive Strategy: Techniques for Analyzing Industries and Competitors* (Free Press, New York, 1980).

5

Smart, Simple, Selective

God plays dice with the Universe. But they're loaded dice. And the main objective is to find out by what rules they were loaded and how we can use them for our own ends.

Joseph Ford[1]

I. SMART MEANS SELECTIVE

Many folk think that strategy is about thinking big, about grand plans, dreaming great dreams, inventing stretch goals, conquering new frontiers, and generally behaving like the corporate equivalent of Moses, Attila the Hun, Alexander the Great, Julius Caesar, Napoleon Bonaparte, John F. Kennedy and Martin Luther King, all rolled into one supercharged and superhuman leader.

If strategy was really like this, very few organizations could muster a single strategist. Yet the good news is that smart strategists require neither charisma nor unusual vision. Of course, it's important to be able to see the big picture. But the big picture in any particular business may sometimes be less important than the small pictures.

Smart people know that good strategy comes from thinking small as well as big, selectively as well as comprehensively, about the present as well as the future, and about what the world is telling you as well as what you should tell the world.

The betting odds are screwed up

Joseph Ford is right: God does load the dice. The world is predictably unbalanced. The smart strategist looks at how God is loading the dice, here and now. If you know how the dice are loaded, you can start to win big time. And it is *your* dice, and your company's dice, that God is loading.

Over a hundred years ago, an obscure Italian professor, working in a Swiss university, made one of the most important and least celebrated discoveries in the history of the world's thinking.

Vilfredo Pareto, one of the smartest people to have on your side for strategy and indeed for helping you run your entire life, found that a small minority of causes or inputs to any event were usually, and predictably, responsible for creating most of that result. Pareto's discovery has been simplified into the *80/20 Principle*,[3] which is that roughly 80% of a goal can be achieved with only 20% of the effort you'd need to

> The 80/20 Principle and chaos theory both tell us that, in any system, few things really matter. What are the few market segments, customers, competitors and skills within our company that really do matter and are the key to our success?

Smart things to say about strategy

reach 100% of the goal. Put another way, the 80/20 Principle says that 20% of anything really matters, and 80% of it doesn't.

Only a few things ever matter much

The 80/20 Principle tell us that in any population, some things are likely to be much more important than others. A rough guide is that 80 per cent of results flow from 20 per cent of causes. The 80/20 Principle is a hypothesis or benchmark, not a magic formula, but it tells us much about the world that we normally wouldn't see.

Take everyday speech. The whole idea of shorthand was based upon Sir Isaac Pitman's discovery that a mere 700 words and their derivatives comprise 80 per cent of our conversation. Since there are more than half a million words in the English language, this means that fewer than 1 per cent of words are used 80 per cent of the time. We could call this an 80/1 principle. It is one of the more extreme illustrations of the 80/20 Principle but a good one: understanding this unbalanced relationship made it possible to record speech quickly.

You can apply the Principle in all sorts of ways. 20 per cent of your clothes are likely to be worn 80% of the time. 20 per cent of your carpets get 80% of the wear. 20 per cent of motorists cause 80 per cent of accidents. 20 per cent of criminals perpetrate 80 per cent of crime and get 80 per cent of the

*SMART PEOPLE
TO HAVE ON
YOUR SIDE:*

*VILFREDO
PARETO
(1848-1923)*

Vilfredo Pareto, called in an obituary 'the bourgeois Karl Marx', was an Italian gentleman, engineer, economist and sociologist who devoted his life to identifying the general rules that shape the modern world. Like Marx, his writings range from punchy and insightful to convoluted and impenetrable. Amongst his claims to fame are the hypothesis that history progressed by a succession of different élites (an inverted class-based theory, where, instead of Marx's proletariat driving progress, it is different and more meritocratic élites that do so), pioneering work on welfare economics, and some astute findings about 'rhythms of sentiment' that drive cycles in business, the stock market, ethics, religion and politics.

Yet Pareto's crowning glory, and the reason smart people absolutely must have Pareto on their side, was his discovery in 1896/97 that there was a consistent and predictably unbalanced relationship between statistical causes and effects. In looking at patterns of wealth and income in England, he found that, at whatever time taken, there was an almost identical and highly skewed relationship between the per cent of people and the per cent of money enjoyed. If 20 per cent of the population had 80 per cent of wealth or income, then 10 per cent would have 65% of the wealth, and 5 per cent would have 50 per cent. Pareto then found similar patterns in all other countries for which he could gather data. Then he found that the relationship worked with other sets of data. In all cases, the world divided into a few important causes or powerful groups, and the mass of weak causes or people.

Pareto never wrote a best-seller and his theories were generally ignored, except by academic economists. But after 1945, his theories were taken up and popularized by Professor George Zipf of Harvard – who proved that 20–30% of any input generally resulted in 70–80% of all relevant output – and by Joseph Juran, the guru behind the Quality Revolution of 1950-90. Pareto's discovery, now generally called the 80/20 Rule or 80/20 Principle, was called by Juran 'the Rule of the Vital Few and the Trivial Many'. All progress, Juran averred, depended on identifying the 'vital few' causes: of quality losses, profits, safety hazards, crime, or whatever one wanted to influence.

Most of the people who have heard about Pareto know next to nothing about him. Many of the things said about him – for example, that he was French-born, that he used the expression '80/20', or that he was a fascist – are simply wrong. If you want to impress people, tell them that Pareto's Principle derived from ideas in his 'Cours d'Economique Politique', published by Lausanne University in 1896/7. If you want to work out a good strategy, for your company or your life, remember that the most powerful 20 per cent of forces usually account for 80 per cent of results. Identify the 20 per cent and make sure you harness them to your cause. Forget about all the rest – it won't make much difference.

There is a best-seller called *The 80/20 Principle*, written by Richard Koch. Modesty forbids me to mention how excellent this book is, but *Business Age* comments that 'through multiple examples, and a punchy down-to-earth commentary, Koch offers the first really useful advice we've seen in a management book for years.' The 80/20 Principle also shows how Pareto's insights can be directed at personal success and happiness and even used to create a better society.

loot. 20 per cent of what you do, at work and outside, achieves 80 per cent of your valued results.

The smart strategist's secret weapon

What, you may reasonably ask, has this got to do with strategy? Very little, you might think, if you read the standard works on strategy, which almost never refer to Vilfredo Pareto or the 80/20 Principle. But smart people know that the 80/20 Principle gives you terrific insights into strategy. You could even say that the 80/20 Principle, while claiming a tiny percentage – well under 20% – of all thinking about strategy, yet manages to produce more than 80 per cent of all useful thinking about strategy.

'80 per cent of value in strategy can be derived from the 80/20 Principle. If companies can find the 20 per cent of things that they do really well, where customers love them, and reward the firm by giving it 80 per cent of its profits, the strategy should be simple. Do more of that 20 per cent, and other similar things.'

How come? Well, something like 80 per cent of your company's products probably only account for 20 per cent of its sales. This means that 20 per cent of the products produce 80 per cent of the sales.

And it's a safe bet that most of your sales come from a small minority of your customers. And – here is the really interesting proposition – that 80 per cent of your profits come from 20 per cent of your business.

If you can define the golden 20 per cent cleverly enough – these products to these customers – it probably will be producing 70 or 80 per cent of your profits. And if *this* is true, it follows that you could increase your profits roughly 50% simply by doubling this golden 20 per cent of your business to 40 per cent of your business, even if all the other business disappeared!

Beating God's odds – a story of God and dog

Imagine that there are five greyhounds in a race, each thought to have an equal chance. If the bookmakers took no profit, each dog would be priced at four-to-one (4/1), meaning that $1 on the right dog would win $5 ($4 plus your $1 stake back). If you put an equal amount on each dog, you would win back your stake, no less and no more.

Now imagine that, through inside information (knowing a trainer or owning the dog, for example), you knew that the dog in trap 1 had an 80% chance of winning. You've seen the dog run in private trials and it is much faster than its kennel mates. If the bookies are offering 4/1 *against* Dog 1, when the true odds should be 1/5 – five-to-one *on*, meaning that $1 should only win 20 cents, the true expected value, since Dog 1 has only one chance out of five of losing – wouldn't you shovel the bucks on to Dog 1, and feel pretty smug as the traps opened? Of course, in any one race you might still lose, but over the long haul you'd make a fortune, until your trick was rumbled.

Improbable though it may sound, the smart strategist who has Vilfredo Pareto and Joseph Ford on her case can pull off the business equivalent of the greyhound betting coup.

All she needs to do is to find the golden 20 per cent of her business, the 20 per cent that produces 80 per cent of the goodies. The smart executive will have sussed, in her own particular world, how God is loading the dice.

'A company's real strategy is in its book of bets.

'Every company has a strategic direction, because every company has a book of bets.

'What every company does not have, however, is a good strategic direction. Not all beliefs are created equal, and when corporate gamblers bet on the basis of flawed assumptions, their odds of achieving the outcome they seek plummet.'

Eileen C. Shapiro[4]

Smart quotes

SMART PEOPLE
TO HAVE ON
YOUR SIDE:

JOSEPH FORD
AND CHAOS
THEORY

Joseph Ford, an American physicist, organized the first conference on the new science of chaos, in 1977, held in the beautiful lakeside town of Como, at the foot of the Italian Alps. Ford is only one of perhaps a dozen key early discoverers and evangelists of 'chaos' or 'chaos theory', but he more than anyone else was responsible for the 'chaos' name, and supplied the quotation with which we started this book.

What should smart people know about chaos theory, and what's it got to do with strategy? Until recently, most scientists took their model of the universe from Isaac Newton. All phenomena could be analyzed into regular, predictable, and linear relationships. For instance, w leads to x, x and y lead to z, and so on. This world view is very useful and comforting, since individual components can be analyzed in terms of the whole, and cause and effect can always be isolated.

During the past thirty years, most scientists have reluctantly come to realize that this mechanical and linear view of the universe is not wholly true. The sharp and separate view of causes and effects has given way to a more complex and blurred picture, where causes are elusive and interdependent, equilibrium is illusory, chaos is rampant ... and yet, where there is a self-organizing but nonlinear logic lurking behind the apparent mess. According to chaos theory, the universe is wonky, but predictable patterns keep recurring. The universe is unbalanced, because some forces are always much more powerful than others and will exert more influence.

Chaos theory says that small initial causes, that might very well be ignored, can become greatly multiplied and produce unpredicted results. This happens when there are powerful positive feedback loops, though these only apply to a small minority of inputs. Also, 'sensitive dependence on initial conditions' means that what happens first can sometimes have quite disproportionate impact.

All this may seem very theoretical and far removed from strategy, but the smart strategist – unlike most business people, and even most so-called experts on strategy – understands the gist of chaos theory and the brilliant light it sheds on strategy. Here are a few key insights on strategy derived from chaos theory:

- Cause and effect don't work in a simple and linear way. Therefore, an intention to do something is no guarantee of the desired result. Any action is likely to have unintended consequences. Therefore, don't place too much value on planning or plans. Experimentation is often better. What works well, especially if its success is unexpected, should be cherished and expanded, even if the causes of success are unknown.
- Identify the powerful causes. Use these; junk the rest. Chaos theory and the 80/20 Principle give the same insight here, because they are both good models of how the world works.
- If you want to dominate a market, it's always useful and sometimes essential to be first in. The second mover has to be much better and smarter to beat the first mover.
- All unconstrained markets gravitate towards having one dominant supplier and many weaker players, because of the positive feedback loops enjoyed by the leader. Such dominant players should have natural advantages, and, if these are not squandered in excess cost, very high profitability. Therefore, seek unconstrained markets where there is not yet a dominant player and where you can become that dominant player.
- Despite the power of dominance, momentum is more important than position. A new or reinvigorated competitor who is gaining market share fast is always a potent threat. A rapid surge in position indicates that the firm has latched on to some powerful force with positive feedback loops. If you are the challenger, drive forward and seize the day before the powerful force abates. If you are the leader, buy or buy off the challenger.

How does the smart strategist find the Golden 20%?

To find the golden 20 per cent of your business that, we guess, may deliver 80 per cent of the profit, the smart strategist must think small. You must divide up your business into chunks – what we called in Chapter Four

'Whenever I've tried to get executives to break down their profits by competitive segments, they've always told me that it's a waste of time, that there are few real differences in profitability, that they know what these are already, and that even if they had the analysis done, they wouldn't be able to anything about it, because even poor profit segments made a contribution to overheads.

'No doubt they'll tell you the same.

'Ignore them. Persevere. Insist.

'When they've done the sums, they'll be staggered by the differences. The discussion can move to a much higher level.'

'competitive segments' – so that each area where you have a different competitor, or a different competitive position (that is, degree of competitive advantage) is treated separately. If you're unsure how to do this, go back to Chapter Four where it is set out clearly.

Smart quotes

'Every set of published accounts is based on books which have been gently cooked or completely roasted. It is the biggest con-trick since the Trojan horse.'

Ian Griffiths[5]

Now what you've got to do is to look at the profitability of each segment, after the allocation of *all* costs, including all overhead costs.

Your financial chief or accountant should be able to do this for you, but you must specify that all costs must be allocated to each of the segments (e.g. the cost of the sales force according to how much time they spend selling the products in each segment).

Let's assume that the sums have been done based on the following eight segments for a specialist software house:

Segment #	Segment description
1	Software for architects sold in the US
2	Software for architects sold in the rest of the world (ROW)
3	Software for human resource (HR) departments in the US
4	Software for human resource (HR) departments in ROW
5	Software for finance departments in the US
6	Software for finance departments in ROW
7	Software for home personal computers (PCs) in the US
8	Software for home personal computers (PCs) in ROW

The results of the profitability analysis are:

Segment	Revenues	Gross Margin	Costs	Profit	ROS
1	$30m	$15m	$5m	$10m	33%
2	$100m	$30m	$20m	$10m	10%
3	$5m	$2m	$1m	$1m	20%
4	$30m	$5m	$6m	($1m)	(3%)
5	$10m	$5m	$4m	$1m	10%
6	$60m	$10m	$10m	$0m	0%
7	$5m	$2m	$3m	($1m)	(20%)
8	$15m	$2m	$7m	($5m)	(33%)
All	$255m	$71m	$56m	$15m	6%

The smart strategist notes immediately that the sales in America are more profitable than those abroad, and that the best results by product are in software for architects – where her firm is the market leader – and the worst is general software for PCs, where her firm has a tiny market share.

KILLER QUESTIONS

What are the chunks of business that account for only 20 per cent of your sales revenues and yet generate 80 per cent of your profits and cash flow?

Now what does the smart strategist do?

Armed with these profit data, she suggests the following smart changes:

- focus on software for architects and HR departments, where we are the market leaders

- make major efforts to sell more in America, where we make much more money because the prices are higher and our selling costs are so much lower. It also transpires from the detailed data that another reason overseas costs are much higher is that the product demand is not exactly the same. This is a particular problem for financial software, where different countries' accounting systems require continual adaptation and tailoring. In many countries, the leader in financial software turns out to be a national specialist.

- look at reducing our selling costs in the rest of the world (ROW), where we don't have enough volume – and given the competition, are never likely to have – to cover the cost of our sales force and make a decent profit. The answer may be to accept slightly lower prices from the leading distributor in each major overseas market, but cut out most

> Q: Why cut out unprofitable business if it still makes a contribution to overheads, since you would reduce profits by cutting out that business?
> A: The overheads have no right to exist if the business they support is un-profitable.
>
> Smaller and more specialized competitors are in the same market and profitable because they don't have our overheads. If we make the business smaller and more profitable, we won't need the overheads either. If we keep the overheads, and competitors with lower overheads eat more and more of our lunch, the whole firm will be in danger before long.
>
> Tough action now – cutting out the unprofitable business and the associated overheads – leads to a great, profitable future. Inaction and preservation of indefensible overheads leads to no future at all.

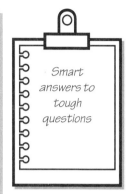

Smart answers to tough questions

of our sales force (the one or two sales people selling to large, national accounts may still be very profitable and worth keeping)

- give up selling home PC software, where others can clearly do it much better and more profitably.

If the company can double sales in the US in architects' and HR software, hang on to its existing sales in architects' software overseas and the business serving American HR departments, get out of the other segments, and cut back its costs accordingly, it would end up with a much smaller yet more profitable business. In our example, the firm, though the market leader, has only about 20 per cent of the architects' and HR software markets in the US, and because it has the better product it is feasible to think of doubling share in a few years. In our illustration the future composition and profits might be:

Segment		Revenue	Profit	ROS
1	Architects (US)	$60m	$20m	33%
2	Architects (ROW)	$100m	$20m	20%
3	HR depts (US)	$10m	$2m	20%
5	Finance depts (US)	$10m	$1m	10%
Total		$180m	$34m	24%

Here turnover has gone down by nearly 30 per cent, but profits have nearly tripled. And the business is much easier to manage, not just because it is smaller, but because it is simpler too.

KILLER QUESTIONS

What would similar profitability analysis of your segments reveal, and why?

The smart strategist will now relate this back to her own business. She'll force herself, and her colleagues, to guess what profitability analysis would show. If different people have different opinions (and they probably will), this is an excellent spur to completing the analysis, so you can see who's right!

Similar analysis should also be performed on *customer* profitability. It will probably show equally striking results.

Smart things
to say about strategy

Serving the most profitable 20 percent of customers – and keeping them consistently delighted – must be a company-wide obsession.

The most loyal customers, those who invariable give you their customer, and those who have been customers the longest, will frequently be very much – perhaps several times – more profitable than other customers (as long as you do the sums right, and allocate the full cost of acquiring and serving each customer).

Smart
examples of
strategy

Too little of anything – space, money, people, revenue – is nearly always better than too much. Too little forces you to be smart. Too much forces you to
be wasteful.[7]

Smart things
to say about
strategy

II. SIMPLE IS BEAUTIFUL

Simple is beautiful. Complex is ugly.

Think of any brilliant strategy that has worked. For example:

- Henry Ford's 'democratization of the automobile' in the first half of
  the twentieth century

- the heavy equipment manufacturer, Komatsu's, strategy of 'encircling
  Caterpillar'

'My effort is in the direction of simplicity. People in general have so little and it costs so much to buy even the barest necessities (let alone the luxuries to which I think everyone is entitled) because nearly everything we do is much more complex than it needs to be. Our clothing, our food, our household furnishing – all could be much simpler than they are now and at the same time be better-looking.'

Henry Ford[8]

Smart things
to say about
strategy

Simple is beautiful. If a strategy isn't simple, it's unlikely to be valuable. If a business isn't simple, it's unlikely to be a winner.

Every business can be simplified, and almost every business can have its value raised dramatically by intelligent simplification.

- Coca-Cola's strategy of having a Coke 'within arm's reach' of every-one on the planet

- Honda's strategy of having the best and cheapest motorcycles, initially in smaller capacities, but then throughout the range – and going for global market leadership

- McDonald's fast-service, family-friendly fast food

- Microsoft's simplification and domination of the PC operating system.

What do all these strategies have in common? Two things. One is that none of them was devised by consultants. The other is that they are all terribly simple, yet terribly ambitious.

Successful strategy is *always* clear and simple. Simple to express. Simple to understand. Even, remarkably, simple to *do*! (Note, though, that simple does not necessarily mean easy. Some simple things can be very difficult to do. But at least everyone knows what the objective is and the whole team's efforts can be orchestrated toward this goal.)

KILLER QUESTIONS

How could we simplify our business in a way that will raise its value by at least 50 per cent?

Perhaps we should not be surprised. If a goal is simple, even a large organization, comprising perhaps hundreds of thousands of people from different backgrounds scattered around the globe, stands a fighting chance of implementing the goal. Each additional element of complexity dramatically knocks out the odds against success.

Researcher Gunter Rommel looked at 39 middle-sized German firms to try to work out why some were much more profitable than others. Guess what he found? The title of his book? *Simplicity Wins*.[9] Simplicity was the *only* characteristic sorting the sheep from the goats. The winning firms sold fewer products to fewer customers and also had fewer suppliers. Their organizations were simpler. So too were their strategies.

KILLER QUESTIONS

- Isn't the strategy we're discussing rather complex?
- Aren't all great strategies simple?
- Can you name an exception?

Another recent survey of 700 US and UK companies by the strategy consultants, The Kalchas Group, found that focused companies – those that participated in one or two primary businesses – performed much better than unfocused companies, having an average 18 per cent

Henry Ford is probably the greatest and most under-rated strategist of all time. Perhaps no industrialist has ever made such a difference to the lives of ordinary people, by giving them, as Gary Hamel has said, 'the precious gift of mobility'.[10]

Before Ford, only very rich people could afford cars. Ford achieved his strategy of 'democratizing the automobile' by dramatically reducing its cost. He achieved this through willpower, volume, the assembly line, and above all through simplification: simplification of strategy, and simplification of the product itself.

How more simple and forceful could a strategy be than Henry Ford's three words in 1909, 'to democratize the automobile'? Try to find a simpler strategy that also has real content; we don't think you will.

Ford knew how to achieve his strategy: by lowering cost. The price of a Ford car in 1916 was 58% lower than in 1908. Ford never doubted that a mass car market existed, if only he could put the automobile's price within reach of the working man; Ford single-handedly created this mass market.

And Ford knew how to lower cost: by simplification. 'I have no use', he exploded, 'for a motor car that has more spark plugs than a cow has teats.' He standardized on one car, the Model T, which he offered 'in any color so long as it's black'.

Today's American managers cut costs by downsizing and screwing the workers. Henry Ford cut costs by superior design, higher volumes, simplification and by extracting higher productivity from workers whom he paid *more*; he introduced the $5 wage, roughly double the going rate at the time.

Ford is an inspiration to the smart strategist. He tells us that it is always possible to cut costs, raise customer value, raise market share, raise the number and pay of staff, raise profits, and explode shareholder value – in short, to change the world for the better, without disadvantaging anyone except competitors – and all through simplification. They will tell you it cannot be done. Henry Ford tells you otherwise.

Al Ries is better known as a marketing expert than as a strategist, but in my book he is one of the smartest strategists on the planet, and one of the easiest and most fun to read too. His message is consistent, clear, and simple. Marketing must focus on one message, one theme, one product line. So too must the corporation itself.

In *Positioning: The Battle for Your Mind* (co-written with Jack Trout), Ries argues that consumers suffer from information overload. To conquer a corner of the mind, the marketing message must be unique, original, simple, consistent and endlessly repeated.

Despite having co-authored several other books – including one with the delightful and insightful title, *Horse Sense: The Key to Success is Finding a Horse to Ride* – the book Al Ries wrote solo, *Focus*, is by far the best. It is also one of the best strategy books of all time and the smart strategist will not long delay buying and reading it.

Ries argues that Corporate America has become unfocused. Companies have extended their product lines, entered whole new businesses, and made acquisitions in unrelated areas. In doing so they have preferred growth to profit, management aggrandizement to shareholder wealth. But now the bloom is off the rose. The errors of unfocusing are evident, and 'never in history have so many chief executives been eased out of their offices by their own boards.'

Globalization, he argues, is the biggest business trend. And globalization should require specialization. 'The larger the market, the more specialization that takes place ... The globalization of business is driving both companies and countries into greater specialization, a trend that is good for everybody.'

'Like amoebas dividing in a petri-dish, business can be viewed as an ever-dividing sea of categories,' he claims. He points to 'the driving force of division', giving cars (from the Model T to today's diversity of categories), computers and many other products. He is scathing about NEC's strategy (praised, you will remember, in Chapter Three by Gary Hamel, in 1990, as a good example of using 'core competencies') of pursuing the convergence of computers and communications ('C&C'). Says Ries:

SMART PEOPLE
TO HAVE ON
YOUR SIDE:

AL RIES

'C&C didn't seem to help NEC. The world's fifth largest maker of telecom equipment, the world's fourth largest maker of computers, and the world's second large maker of semiconductors, NEC makes everything except money. In the past decade, NEC shares have lagged behind the Japanese stock market by 28 per cent.'

Convergence, Ries claims, is a myth. 'Convergence is against the laws of nature ... In biology, the law of evolution holds that new species are created by the division of a single species. Convergence, on the other hand, would have you believe that species are constantly combining, yielding such curiosities as the catdog.'

Ries was one of the first strategists to notice the real significance of the spinoff movement, probably the most important corporate development of the 1990s. 'The surge of spinoffs and sell-offs is proof positive that the age of diversification and the age of conglomerization are finally over. We have entered the age of focus.'

We have indeed. And, obeying his own precept ('if you want to be famous ... own a word in the mind. That's true of an individual; it's also true of a company'), Ries will be forever associated with the new age of focus. Expect him to become a lot more famous!

growth in earnings per share versus 11 per cent for the unfocused, and much higher price/earnings multiples for the focused companies too.

The evidence that focus and simplicity work is overwhelming.

But why is simple beautiful?

For one thing, because the customer can easily identify the company and what it does. This works at the level of branding, where everyone on earth who has any money knows what a Coke is, what a Filofax is, what Mars or Kellogg make, or what Disney or McDonald's stand for. The value in term of free advertising is massive. The strategic value of a good brand may be literally incalculable. The brand may exclude any competitor from the precise niche occupied by the brand.

But any powerful brand can only operate on a very narrow wavelength: not necessarily of one product, but certainly of one set of values, one type of target customer, one character of service, and one type of emotion. For a brand to work well, it must be simple and transmit a simple message.

Smart quotes

'Enlightened capitalism is the *everyday* quest to do more, in a better way, *with less.*'

Barry Gibbons[11]

If simplicity raises customers' awareness, sympathy and clarity with regard to a company and its products or services, simplicity therefore automatically raises sales, lowers the cost of acquiring a customer, lowers the rate at which customers defect to competing products (itself a key source of cost advantage).

Simplicity may also raise average prices without raising costs. Simplicity therefore equals higher profits.

Another powerful reason simplicity works is that simplicity lowers cost and raises quality. Low cost, the smart strategist will recall, is one of the two powerful and versatile source of competitive advantage (the other being differentiation).

Smart quotes

'Powerful ideas are usually utterly simple: "Safety" for Volvo, "Overnight" for Federal Express.'

Al Ries

With lower costs, a firm can price lower than competitors and gain market share. This is turn lowers its costs further, and raises costs for the competitors.

Smart examples of strategy

IBM versus Compaq

'IBM was a $35 billion powerhouse when Compaq was just a sketch on a paper place mat. Yet thirteen years later, Compaq leads IBM in personal computers by a wide margin. Compaq is focused. IBM is not.'

Al Ries

Or the low cost corporation can reinvest in extra quality and know-how, hire the best people, add extra features or service or advertising or sales people – all of which should further compound its lead. The low cost firm can also raise returns to shareholders and lower its cost of capital.

The simple firm – with a simple strategy – and a single product line or service – and a simple structure – this firm can keep increasing its competitive advantage and its lead ... as long as it keeps things simple.

Complexity poisons. Complexity leads to high costs. It engenders mistakes and poor quality. It leads to frustration. It hides incompetence. It weakens resolve. It destroys accountability. Complexity spawns overhead and bureaucracy. *It is not a good idea!*

Smart quotes

'As anyone who has worked in a large bureaucracy knows, most of its energy is used simply reproducing itself. The same is true of the classic modern corporation.

'The weak power structures of the new times are very different. Above all, energies are devoted outwards rather than inwards.'

Geoff Mulgan[12]

The sun versus the laser

'The sun is a powerful source of energy. Every hour the sun washes the earth with billions of kilowatts of energy. Yet with a hat and some sunscreen you can bathe in the light of the sun for hours at a time with few ill effects.

'A laser is a weak source of energy. A laser takes a few watts of energy and focuses them in a coherent stream of light. But with a laser you can drill a hole in a diamond or wipe out a cancer.

'When you focus a company, you create the same effect. You create a powerful, laserlike ability to dominate a market. That's what focusing is all about.

'When a company becomes unfocused, its loses its power. It becomes a sun that dissipates its energy over too many products and too many markets.'

Al Ries[13]

The smart strategist knows that, both for himself and his company, it is much easier to do one thing well, economically and fast, than to do several. If he does ten things, he will end up spending more time and mental effort switching between tasks. The gaps will rule. This is one good reason why focus and simplicity are so effective.

III. SIMPLICITY, FOCUS AND CORPORATE STRUCTURE

If simple organizations are better than complex ones, and there is clear advantage in having a corporation focused on one single type of business activity, wouldn't the smart strategist expect that most companies would be Single Business Corporations (SBCs)?

Yet as you survey the corporate landscape, what do you see? Well, you do see some very big and very successful SBCs, like Hertz, Coca-Cola, McDonald's, Microsoft, Goldman Sachs (the investment bankers), or Intel Corporation (the computer chip makers), as well as a host of successful small and medium-sized SBCs. No surprise there.

But when you look at the typical large corporation, you see a multi-business corporation (MBC).

> Smart examples of strategy

Coke versus Pepsi

'No two companies illustrate the power of a focus better than PepsiCo Inc and The Coca-Cola Company ...

'Pepsi, the larger company, is worth $44 billion, and Coca-Cola, the smaller company, is worth $93 billion, more than twice as much. Per dollar of sales, Coca-Cola is worth almost four times as much as PepsiCo. That's the power of a focus.'

Al Ries

The problem for Pepsi was that it was a diversified corporation, owning restaurants (which often competed with its customers for Pepsi-Cola), snack foods and a wide range of beverage brands in addition to its cola. In contrast, The Coca-Cola Corporation is just a beverage company and is focused on Coca-Cola.

Since Al Ries made these comments, PepsiCo has sold some of its non-beverage interests, but it still much more diversified than Coca-Cola ... and is still losing the battle.

Smart examples of strategy

Toys 'R' Us

'Today the company has 618 stores in the United States and sells 22 per cent of all the toys in the country. Ironically, Toys 'R' Us started as a children's furniture store to which founder Charles Lazarus added toys ...

'[Then] he threw out the furniture and opened another, larger store with discount toys only. In other words, he narrowed the focus to toys. How unusual and how effective ...

'There are five steps in the Toys 'R' Us formula:

1.   Narrow the focus
2.   Stock in depth
3.   Buy cheap
4.   Sell cheap
5.   Dominate the category.

'Pretty simple, huh?'

Al Ries

How come? Do simplicity and focus work for small and medium-sized corporations, but not for their larger brethren? Does overhead, so corrosive at the level of an individual business, suddenly become useful – or potentially useful – when applied to a variety of businesses? Or is the corporate form of the MBC deceptive? Do several small and focused businesses actually live and prosper under the corporate umbrella of the typical large multi-business corporation?

Conclusion

To answer these questions, we enter in Chapter Six the mysterious world of corporate strategy. Here we will find, beneath the apparently solid surface of successful corporations, a turbulent world, a constant battle between value creation and value destruction. Come with me now into this exhilarating arena.

Notes

1 For those interested in chaos theory and Joseph Ford, see the classic book *Chaos: Making A New Science* by James Gleik (Little, Brown & Co., New York, 1987). Those who enjoy this book may like to graduate to recent work on Complexity, for which by far the best introduction is the highly readable *Complexity* by M. Mitchell Waldrop (Simon & Schuster, New York, 1992, now also available in Penguin).

2 1654–1734, British writer and doctor

3 Richard Koch, *The 80/20 Principle* (US: Currency Doubleday, New York, 1998; Rest of World: Nicholas Brealey, London, revised edition 1998).

4 *Fad Surfing in the Boardroom* (Capstone, Oxford, 1997).

5 British forensic accountant, in his splendid whistle-blowing book, *Creative Accounting*.

6 I am grateful to Al Ries for the examples and quotations culled from his path-breaking book *Focus* (HarperCollins, London, 1996). The sequel, *Future Focus* by Al Ries and Theodore B. Kinni (Capstone,

Oxford, 1999) is a fascinating exploration of the ingredients of 21st century corporate success, and the companies most likely to exemplify it.

7 Adapted from Robert Townsend, *Up The Organization*.

8 In the 1920s.

9 Harvard Business School Press, Cambridge, 1996.

10 Stuart Crainer and Gary Hamel, *The Ultimate Business Library* (Capstone, Oxford, 1997), pp. 99–103.

11 Barry Gibbons, *If You Want to Make God Really Laugh Show Him Your Business Plan* (Capstone, Oxford, 1998).

12 Very smart contemporary British political philosopher. See his excellent book, *Politics in an Antipolitical Age* (Blackwell Publishers, Oxford, 1995).

13 The opening words of *Focus*.

6

The Joy of Corporate Strategy

'You see things; and you say why? *But I dream things that never were; and I say* why not?'

George Bernard Shaw[1]

The good news

The essence of corporate strategy is putting new dreams for value creation into action. Corporate strategy is about creating and growing a whole business, an entire corporation, and as such is the most exciting and un-bounded part of business life. Corporate strategy answers three questions:[2]

1. What businesses do we want to be in? Where should we invest our resources? And what form should this investment take – total owner-ship, minority holdings, joint ventures, alliances or franchising?

2. How do we want to structure and run the businesses?

3. How can we create value in a way that no other corporation can?

All great and successful companies have found unique answers to these questions. All the great corporations of the future will find their own fresh answers.

Why good corporate strategy is rare

Most companies today do not have very convincing answers to the three questions. This is not surprising, since the theory of corporate strategy has not been very well developed. Most of the answers supplied by academics, consultants and business people themselves have proved to be flawed.

There is mounting evidence that corporate strategy – at least, of the type typically practised today – may frequently do more harm than good.

Why have the theory and practice of corporate strategy been problematic?

Smart quotes

The follies and misfortunes of earlier corporate strategy

Corporate strategy has a symbiotic relationship with the emergence of the Multi-Business Corporation (MBC) and with the associated growth of Head Offices (the 'corporate level' to match the 'corporate strategy') staffed by professional managers.

Before the twentieth century, nearly all companies were in just one single line of business. They were Single Business Corporations (SBCs). The nineteenth century SBCs were very largely owned and run by family entrepreneurs.

Smart quotes

'The implication of research on unsuccessful diversification, corporate breakups, and value gaps is that billions of dollars of value are destroyed or suppressed each year by bad corporate-level decisions.'

Goold, Campbell and Alexander

In the first half of the twentieth century, there were two transformations. First, professional managers began to replace family owners as the people who ran businesses from day to day. Second, the structure of the modern corporation changed. Those at the top, whether owners or hired managers, could not cope with the volume of decisions rising to them. The solution, pioneered by the largest companies such as General Motors and DuPont, was to divisionalize, to delegate most decisions to the new divisions. In short, to invent the MBC. Effectively, each division became its own business, with the top corporate level confining itself to the most important investment decisions and relations with the providers of funds: with bankers and increasingly also with the stock market.

Smart quotes

It may be a coincidence but America started losing international competitiveness from the moment that the modern MBC was born.'

David Sadtler, Andrew Campbell and Richard Koch[6]

Divisionalization, from the 1920s, created the MBC. It also created a new level – the corporate level, the modern head office and other levels of central overhead, divisional and regional head offices. When business strategy began to emerge, it naturally fell into the same distinction. Those at the head offices pursued 'corporate' strategy, while those in the divisions and sub-divisions concerned themselves with 'business unit' strategy.

And so, up until the 1980s, the die of modern capitalism was cast – cast in the mould of divisionalized, diversified corporations, increasingly funded not by families but by the stock market, increasingly managed not by owners or industry experts but by professional general managers without a real ownership stake in the business, financed by anonymous investment institutions, and accountable, in practice, to no-one.

In 1949, 24 per cent of the Fortune 500 companies were divisionalized; by 1959 51 per cent; by 1969, 80 per cent. With divisionalization came diversification: by 1969, 44 per cent of all the divisionalized companies had diversified. By the 1980s it became almost impossible to find a large American company that had not diversified, as the pursuit of growth and synergy – one of the first inventions of the new corporate strategy of the 1960s – became the new corporate religion. The SBC was passé. The MBC ruled. Even Coca-Cola, for more than a century the archetypal and very successful SBC, succumbed. In 1982 Coca-Cola bought Columbia Pictures, and soon after the Taylor Wine Company.

Corporate strategists celebrated and encouraged these initiatives. They praised the general managers, trained by the business schools, able to shift easily from one industry to another. They praised diversification. They praised synergy between existing businesses and new ones. They invented 'portfolio planning' techniques for those at the centre to shift cash and resources from one division to another. By 1979, 45 per cent of the Fortune 500 companies were using portfolio planning.

It didn't work

By the 1980s, the failures of divisionalization, the MBC, diversification, portfolio planning, synergy, the 'professional' general manager without industry expertise, and the whole theory and practice of corporate strategy had become painfully apparent, even to the practitioners and theorists themselves.

The problem of the diversified MBC was highlighted by the corporate raiders of the 1980s. Not even the largest companies were immune from attack, as Carl Icahn, T. Boone Pickens, KKR, the leveraged buyout specialist, and many other raiders proved that they could pay large premiums

Smart quotes

'I studied the diversification records of 33 large, prestigious US companies over the 1950–86 period and found that most of them had divested many more acquisitions than they had kept. The corporate strategies of most companies have dissipated instead of created shareholder value ... By taking over companies and breaking them up, corporate raiders thrive on failed corporate strategies.'

Michael E. Porter[7]

over the stock market value of diversified corporations and then break them up, realizing huge profits.

The 1990s have seen further reversals of the previously inexorable trend towards larger and more diversified corporations. Mounting evidence that more focused corporations tend to perform better than diversified ones has not been ignored. The dollar value of US spinoffs has accelerated throughout the 1990s, as MBCs have broken themselves up into two, three or more new, more focused corporations. European corporations are increasingly joining the breakup movement. Japanese and other Asian conglomerates have not yet followed suit.

What does all this mean for corporate strategy? Do we understand why many MBCs went astray? Was the MBC itself a mistake? Should all MBCs become SBCs? Should head offices be abolished? Is corporate strategy itself part of the problem rather than the solution? Is there a theory that can explain both the successes and the failures of corporate strategy, and that can give practical guidance to those running MBCs and their strategists?

The theory of value destruction

Value Destruction theory states that in the MBC the corporate centre – the headquarters plus the divisional and/or regional head offices – is genetically predisposed to destroy more value than it adds. The centre will almost certainly add value, probably large amounts of it. But it may well destroy more value than it adds. This is without regard to the professionalism, motivation, skill and dedication of those at the centre. Excellent managers at the centre may even destroy more value than mediocre executives.

'In contrast to the businesses, the parent [the centre] does not have external customers and generates costs but no revenues...

It follows that primary wealth generation takes place only at the business level, and that the parent [centre] must work through its businesses to create value ... Would they perform better or worse as stand-alone entities?

For the parent [centre] to destroy value ... cannot be acceptable.'

Goold, Campbell and Alexander

The theory points out that centres of corporations are odd things. Centres are intermediaries between the primary level of wealth generation – the individual businesses that do have customers and competitors – and the providers of funds: investors and banks.

In most cases the individual businesses could exist perfectly well on their own, without the centre. They could obtain their funds from business angels, venture capitalists, bankers, and/or the stock market.

So, in pure economic terms, the centre has to justify its existence by adding value. And this must be *net* value added – the centre must add more value than it subtracts.

The centre is thus an optional extra. True, it owns the businesses. But it need not. If the centre did not exist it would not be necessary to invent it.

Centres are therefore a good idea *only* if they add more value than they destroy. This is true both of an individual business, and of multi-business corporations as a whole. The centre of any company should certainly not

- Do our headquarters and other support offices add more value than they subtract?
- Would our individual business units vote to retain 'the centre', if they were given a genuinely free choice between the status quo and becoming independent companies without the centre?

exist unless it adds net value. The way we organize most of big business into MBCs is not a good idea, if abolishing MBCs and having a larger number of smaller and more focused corporations would provide society with more economic value.

Now, having set up the issue this way, value-destruction theory tests whether individual centres, and the majority of centres of MBCs, can pass the test of adding more value than they subtract.

Sure, the theory says, centres *do* typically add a lot of value. This is why they seem sensible things to have. There are nearly always cost reductions from combining into one group ... Typically, the squeeze can be put on suppliers, both because of extra volume of purchases, and because the new group has more information about better and cheaper alternatives. Since for most companies the cost of bought-in goods and services comprises roughly a half of total cost, even small improvements in purchasing can lead to large increases in profit margins. The combined company, being bigger, will be able to spread its overhead costs over greater volumes

Smart things to say about strategy

Unless the centre adds more value than it subtracts, and unless the business units would freely vote to retain the centre, it should go. In either case, economic value would be released by giving the businesses their independence.

> It's easy to see the centre adds value to its businesses. And it's easy to ignore how the centre subtracts value too, especially if you live at the centre.
>
> But would an honest, objective observer think the value added is greater than the value subtracted, or vice versa?

Smart things to say about strategy

and therefore cut the costs. There may not be a need for two French offices, for two sales forces in each territory, for two lots of buyers, trainers, treasury experts, legal staffs, and so on. The cost of borrowing may be lower for a bigger group, or the stock market rating higher (thereby lowering the cost of equity capital).

So if all these cost savings add up to more than the cost of the new centre, it seems a good deal.

Beyond lowering costs, the centre can add great value to its businesses. It can add wisdom and experience, improving decisions. It can attract higher calibre executives, offering superior careers and training. It can challenge executives to stretch their goals and profitability beyond past levels. It can promulgate superior formulae, tried and tested ways of running the business more effectively, serving customers better and retaining them longer, subtly raising margins, and discouraging competitors. It can persuade the businesses to focus on their most profitable customers and products, to leave marginal or loss-making businesses, or to sell surplus assets.

The centre of a large company can also help its business units develop new products and get them to market quicker than a stand-alone company could. The combined group may have better customer intelligence and may provide funds quicker and more fully than a stand-alone firm, doing the rounds of financiers, could possibly manage on its own. The centre can encourage more aggressive expansion at the right time, pick better CEOs and other key executives. Centres can add value in myriad ways. Good centres can add tremendous value. Even poor centres add some value.

So far, the theory would appear to endorse the value of centres. But here comes the twist. Yes, the theory says, centres add lots of value. *But they also destroy a lot, usually in less evident, but no less important, ways than they add value. Both in theory and in practice, it is possible to point to massive value destruction by centres. And there is generally more value destruction than value creation. On balance, therefore, unless they can improve their performance dramatically, most centres of MBCs should go, most MBCs should go.*

The theory can prove the existence of net value destruction empirically, by referring to the spinoff or breakup phenomenon.

Breakups – also known as spinoffs, de-mergers and unbundlings – are a fantastically important development, perhaps the most significant departure in corporate life since the MBC itself was invented.

Smart quotes

'To argue the logic of the breakup, we need to argue for the existence of value destruction. And, since we posit that the value created by a group is often substantial; and that the net benefits of breakups are, in most cases, very substantial; we have to argue that the amounts of value destroyed by many MBCs are more substantial still.

'It so happens that this is the case.'

Sadtler, Campbell and Koch

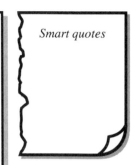
Smart quotes

'Corporate America and corporate Britain are in the midst of an epidemic that will change the face of capitalism. In an unprecedented whirlwind of self-dismemberment, companies that used to believe that big is beautiful are splitting into two, three or more separate companies.

'The epidemic is good news. It will be the greatest wealth-producing change in our lifetimes.'

Sadtler, Campbell and Koch

In the 1990s, American companies breaking themselves up have included some of the biggest and proudest MBCs: Anheuser-Busch, Baxter International, Corning, Dun & Bradstreet, Dial, General Mills, General Motors, Grace, ITT, Lilly, Marriott, 3M, Pacific Telesis, Ralston Purina, Sears and Tenneco. British companies breaking-up have included BAT, British Gas, Courtaulds, ECC, Hanson, ICI, Lonrho, Racal, and Thorn EMI. Breakups in Continental Europe include Lufthansa, Sandoz, Sonae, Chargeurs, Hoechst, and many other smaller corporations. In the US breakups have grown in value every year since 1992 and are now the most important single source of disposals and larger than the 1980s leveraged buyout (LBO) movement at its peak.

Breakups release economic value. A careful study of spinoffs by JP Morgan, the international investment bank, showed that the average spinoff performed 25 per cent better than the average of its stock market peers during the first 18 months after breakup, and was still on a clearly rising trend. For the smaller spinoffs – those with an initial market value of $200m or less – the outperformance was a staggering 45 percent.

Value-destruction theory points to the evidence that independent companies perform better than those in a group, and concludes that the existence

'In a short time, breakup has become a major force, growing with apparently relentless vigour...

'The evidence that breakups work could scarcely be clearer ... the average spin-off performed 25 per cent better than the stock market in the first 18 months after breakup.'

Sadtler, Campbell and Koch

of the centre or the group *must* have been destroying more value than it added. Since nothing else was changed by the spinoff, this must be so.

And since we have observed that groups add a lot of value, if the *net* result of ending the group is a large increase in value, simple math dictates that the amount of value destruction by the centre or the grouping must be the net amount of value released by the breakup (on average 25 per cent or 45 per cent for the smaller spinoffs) *plus* the value being added by the group (unquantified, but generally considerable). Putting independent companies into MBCs must therefore entail, typically, massive value destruction.

The theory then seeks to explain and document such value destruction. The Ashridge researchers documented four types:

- executive influence

- linkage initiatives/synergy

- central staffs

- portfolio development.

Smart things to say about strategy

The smart strategist should be aware of all four value destroyers and look for their possible existence in her organization.

Value destroyer #1: executive influence

All centres powerfully influence the businesses they own. The centre allocates funds, guides strategy, sets budgets, promotes or fires executives. The Ashridge research evidence, surprisingly, is that the centre's executive influence is usually heavily net negative. It takes away more value than it supplies. Why? Look out for the following danger signals:

Lack of fit between centre and its businesses
If the centre does not really understand all its businesses as well as those who run them, it will tend to make less good decisions than they would.

This is most acute where the people at the centre come from a different business. Paradoxically, the worst damage can arise when the businesses appear only *slightly* different. In this case, the centre feels confident overruling the business, yet the confidence may be totally misplaced.

Take oil and minerals. Similar businesses, huh? So when, in the 1980s, three well run oil businesses – Shell, Exxon, and BP – bought minerals businesses, you'd expect them to be able to bring some of their experience to bear and to exert a positive influence on their minerals divisions.

> **Smart things
> to say about strategy**
>
> If a new business looks familiar, beware! The hidden differences may be more important than the evident similarities.

Badly wrong. The oil companies' mineral businesses averaged minus 17 per cent return on sales during the 1980s, at the same time the independent minerals companies averaged ten per cent *positive*. So what went wrong? In oil, spending money on exploration is a good route to superior profits. In minerals, searching for new deposits is less important than joint venturing with companies who already have low-cost mines. The oil companies took their oil experience and made the minerals companies overinvest in exploration. Despite superficial similarities, oil and minerals are really two different worlds.

The 10 per cent versus 100 per cent paradox
A group CEO with ten divisions reporting to him will spend, on average, only ten per cent of her time on any one division. A divisional CEO will spend 100 per cent of her time. Therefore, the group CEO must be ten times smarter to take better decisions. Enough said!

The truth possession and perversion paradox
For the centre to take better decisions, it must be better informed than the division. Yet most of the centre's information comes from the division. This information is nearly always slanted in ways that makes it less accurate and less helpful.

Subsidiary executives probably won't pass on unfiltered truth. There may be a crisis they want to conceal or downplay. They may exaggerate good news, in the hope of being rewarded with more investment or higher pay.

Notoriously, budgeting turns into a negotiating game rather than a mutual exploration of business prospects.

Even without perversion of truth, those close to customers and competitors are almost bound to make better decisions than the generals at one remove. As the Soviet empire showed, bureaucratic decisions at the top are usually wrong.

The alienation syndrome
You work harder and smarter if you control your own destiny. A large corporate without alienation is like a long marriage without quarrels: theoretically possible but never observed.

The insulation syndrome
Why is it that management teams who have just completed a buyout (an MBO or LBO) suddenly find that they can cut costs, raise sales and do without certain assets? Because they really want to and really need to. Because the money, for the first time, is really *theirs*. Within a large corporation you are insulated against misfortune, and imperfectly accountable and motivated.

KILLER QUESTIONS

Do you really expect people to use corporate cash the same way they'd use their own cash? Do you?

Value destroyer #2: linkage initiatives/synergy

Synergy is the exploitation of links between 'sister' businesses to create extra value. Yet normally synergy is a mirage and the attempt to create it is more trouble than it's worth.

Corporate centre bias
In life, you find what you look for. Executives at the centre want to find synergies: they justify the group. So they find synergy. But it's often a mirage.

The benefits may possibly be real; but the hidden costs of realizing synergy may exceed the benefits.

Enlightened self-interest paradox

Those who run businesses are always searching for new partners, new transactions, new alliances. If there is benefit from synergy within a group, why won't self-interest of the principals identify it?

Perhaps only if past clumsy attempts to encourage synergy have left a sour taste in the mouth. Why do sister companies often find it more difficult dealing with each other than with outside partners? It can only be because they have to deal with noncommercial baggage, with authority and with personal obligations.

Paradoxically, genuine synergy, within a total economy, may be greater if all companies were independent than if they were organized into a smaller number of groupings.

Value destroyer #3: central services

In most MBCs there are central staff services offering advice and guidance in many areas – finance, tax, legal, human resources, research, engineer-

'No question: managers find it hard to create synergy from the business units under their command. Our research findings are clear. Precious few are the managers who have responded to us with: "Ah yes. Co-ordinating business units. Let me tell you how we do this. It's pretty straightforward. We ..." '

Andrew Campbell and Michael Goold[8]

'These service departments and functions are a well-documented source of problems. In most companies they are under attack and for good reason. The policies they impose on the portfolio are frequently inappropriate, the services they provide unresponsive, and their influence on the corporate psyche disempowering.'

Sadtler, Campbell and Koch

ing, procurement, public relations, sometimes even cleaning and staff feeding.

Value destroyer #4: portfolio development

This should mean using the cash and know-how of the corporation to grow and reshape it. In other words, to answer the first question we posed, at the start of this Chapter: What businesses do we want to be in, and how should we invest our resources?

Many companies have prospered and achieved fame and greatness by answering this question well. Yet many other companies grow in their niches to a certain point and then surrender the gains through inappropriate portfolio development – typically through diversification. And many once-great companies have squandered their accumulated – and often undeclared – surpluses on acts of great corporate folly, especially value-destroying acquisitions.

Smart quotes

'The concentration of power is what always precedes the destruction of human initiative; and, therefore, of human energy.'

Woodrow Wilson[9]

If failing companies use their accumulated clout to acquire better and faster-growing companies, and then destroy value in them, this causes a real subtraction of value, not just from individual corporations, but also from the economy as a whole.

False market in acquisitions

Research has proved that, on average, acquisitions do not add value to the acquirer. In about half the cases, the acquirer loses substantially, sometimes disastrously. A substantial 'acquisition premium' is paid and needs to be recouped through 'synergy' or other benefits. Typically, value *is* added. But value is also subtracted. The net change is usually not enough to justify the acquisition premium. Even worse, the hidden costs of acquisition, especially if it involves greater complexity and diversity, are likely to emerge fully only over long periods of time, and are unlikely to be attributed correctly to the acquisition.

What creates the false market in acquisitions is that there are more managers of large companies who want to make acquisitions than there are corresponding managers who want to be acquired. Yet if executives were motivated predominantly to increase shareholder wealth, it would be the other way round. The CEOs of MBCs would be falling over themselves to be acquired, or, if no-one would offer an acquisition premium, to break themselves up into more than one new corporation.

Smart quotes

'The capital markets will increase the pressure on companies to sell assets for which they are not the best owners. If a company is unwilling to spin off those assets or to sell them, then someone will acquire the company and do it anyway.'

Lowell Bryan and Diana Farrell[10]

It follows that the leaders of MBCs are systematically destroying wealth by the pursuit of acquisition-led growth and by refusing to dismantle existing MBCs. The only exception is when acquisitions are made specifically to break up a company into its constituent parts and/or to sell the parts to the highest bidder.

Conclusion on value-destruction theory

We've now completed our whirlwind tour of value-destruction theory. The smart strategist should have picked up many leading indicators of danger and many things to avoid and if possible reverse. Corporate strategy is a tricky area. But it would be wrong to stop here, on a negative note. There *is* a right way to approach corporate strategy.

The right approach to developing corporate strategy

It's high time to pull together practical advice on how to develop a good corporate strategy. Remember that corporate strategy involves answering the three questions posed at the start of this Chapter, so when you have completed the steps below, see if you can then convincingly answer the three questions. There are four steps:

1. Find your value-creation insights

2. Define how the centre is going to add value

3. Focus on heartland businesses

4. Decide whether to restructure or breakup.

SMART PEOPLE
TO HAVE ON
YOUR SIDE:

THE ASHRIDGE
STRATEGISTS:
MARCUS
ALEXANDER,
ANDREW
CAMPBELL
AND MICHAEL
GOOLD

The Ashridge strategists have specialized in corporate as opposed to business unit strategy, and specifically they have appropriated the question of how to structure, lead and strategize for multibusiness companies (MBCs). They astutely observed, back in the early 1980s, that business unit strategy had much better theory than corporate strategy, and that with the failure of 'synergy' and 'portfolio development' techniques there was a hugely important vacuum to fill. To switch metaphors, they are slowly, steadily, tenaciously and rather successfully ascending their mountain. They will get there before they die.

Andrew Campbell is a loud, warm, impulsive Scot who is a former consultant with McKinsey & Company. Michael Goold is a tall, youthful-but-stooping, donnish and precise Englishman who was an intellectual adornment to the Boston Consulting Group in its first years in London (in the early to mid 1970s); his most memorable achievement at BCG was writing the report on the British motorcycle industry, or what remained of it, in 1975–6.

Mike Goold went from BCG to the London Business School to launch a research project into decision-making in large MBCs. McKinsey were supporters of the project and in 1987 Goold and Campbell teamed up to found the Ashridge Strategic Management Centre with the same focus. They were later joined by Marcus Alexander, a brilliant Brit, also from McKinsey.

Their first work, based on the London Business School research, came in 1987. *Strategies And Styles* by Goold and Campbell was a pioneering work, in that it was the first to categorize different central styles – Strategic Planning, Strategic Control, and Financial Control – and took an admirably open-minded view of the merits and demerits of each. It concluded that there was no best style, but that different types of company, competitive position and leader were better fitted to each style. *Strategies And Styles* is rather a tame book. It is largely superseded by the much feistier and conclusive 1994 landmark, *Corporate-Level Strategy: Creating Value in the Multibusiness Company*.

Here Goold, Campbell and Alexander originated both Value Destruction theory and Parenting theory. If Value Destruction was rife within MBCs, a new approach was required to steer the corporate strategist and CEO toward net value creation.

The book elaborated the metaphor of the 'parent company', also known as the 'centre'. Although the parent owns the subsidiary divisions, it should base its role not on authority and ownership but on expertise and economic value-added.

The trio also invented the useful concept of 'Parenting Advantage'. This is like competitive advantage, but refers to the activity of the centre rather than to the operating businesses. Unless the parent company is creating value from owning the businesses, it should not do so.

The most valuable part of *Corporate-Level Strategy* for the corporate strategist is the Framework for Parenting Advantage and the examples of successful corporate strategies. Three indispensable features of successful parents are described:

- value creation insights
- distinctive parenting characteristics
- heartland businesses

and, for the smart strategist, defining these for your corporation is vital.

Value-creation insights are uncommon formulae for better performance in specific businesses. Value-creation insights are quite similar to what Peter Drucker calls 'the theory of the business' and defines as 'the assumptions about what a company gets paid for'. Andrew Campbell and Marcus Alexander have refined the idea in a recent article:

'Insights into value creation ... allow one to discover superior ways of creating value. These insights normally focus on practical issues and point to new ways of doing things ... Sometimes the insights are grand ideas to reconfigure the company or the industry completely. More commonly, they are discoveries that some process can be performed by fewer people or that a segment

of customers require a new service. Such insights often come from line or operating managers who may not be fully aware of their significance.'

Distinctive Parenting Characteristics are the way that the centre adds value; specific ways in which the centre ensures that the total corporation can exploit the value creation insights.

Heartland Businesses are not simply core businesses; rather they are businesses where the centre's insights and skills are particularly pertinent. Unless there is this fit, the business is not in the heartland and the parent should not own it.

Thus for an effective corporate strategy, there must be value creation insights, distinctive parenting characteristics, and only heartland businesses: and all three must fit with the other two.

Finally, we should mention *Breakup! When Large Companies are Worth More Dead than Alive* (1997). *Breakup!* was not an official Ashridge book but was written by David Sadtler, Andrew Campbell and me as a 'pop' exposition of the value destruction theory. It went further than Mike Goold and Marcus Alexander wanted in condemning the MBC as an institution and the book is unusual in containing a disclaimer explicitly exempting the Ashridge Strategic Management Centre from any responsibility:

Breakup! draws deeply on the Ashridge research, but there are differences ... we present both a more provocative and a looser message than that contained in the Ashridge work. This is not primarily a research-based book. It is a collection of observations, ideas, and beliefs. We are not seeking precision and proof. We are seeking insight and implication. This is a popular rather than a theoretical book ... Our views about the pervasiveness of value destruction and the implications for the future are our own, not those of Ashridge.'

The work of Alexander, Campbell and Goold writing together always carries the imprimatur of academic quality and intellectual respectability. The ASMC brand may innovate, but it guarantees deep thought and rigorous logic based on solid research. It is also appropriately positive, so much so that Gary Hamel has observed, rather tartly, that 'in writing the definitive book on corporate strategy, Goold, Alexander and Campbell gave hope to corporate bureaucrats everywhere. Maybe, occasionally, it really was possible for the corporate level to add value.'

1. Find your value-creation insights

You simply *must* have these. They must be superior ways of doing business: better, cheaper, faster, or nicer. They must be unusual in your markets; if they are or become commonplace, they're useless in giving you the edge. Fundamentally the value-creation insights relate to competitive advantage in particular business units, but represent a way of doing business that can be generalized over many different segments.

Because the value-creation insights relate to 'real' businesses, the corporate centre may not be the best place to discover them. If it is, it will be because the chief executive or others at the centre used to work in real business and discovered the insights there.

If the centre doesn't have the insights, fear not; you can always go to the businesses to see what insights enable superior performance. The insights do not have to be articulated fully, or at all, for them to be there. The smart strategist will mine and refine the insights by observing where the businesses are most successful. This is one of the most creative, valuable and rewarding tasks that the corporate strategist can undertake.

The value-creation insights should be few and powerful. They must be capable of being applied by some appropriate intervention by the centre, for which the centre is well qualified (the distinctive parenting characteris-

ABB

Value creation
insights

Most European engineering businesses have been
    strong in their niches in Europe but have not sought
    to dominate global niches. The latter is a superior,
    more profitable strategy.
Many engineering businesses have too wide a
    product line and seek sales even at the expense of
    profit margins.
A more focused and commercial approach has great
    benefit

Distinctive
parenting
characteristics

Ability to combine decentralized small business units
    into a global network
Ability to make acquisitions and improve their
    performance rapidly:
- hack out overhead costs
- focus on customer needs
- focus on high profit segments and raising margins
  in low profit segments
- simplification

Heartland
businesses

Engineering-intensive, electrotechnical businesses,
    needing complex integration into systems, for large
    industrial or government customers

Source: adapted from *Corporate-Level Strategy* by Goold, Campbell &
Alexander

tics). And they must be capable of being applied across all the businesses, which are therefore heartland businesses. If the value-creation insights do not meet these requirements, either the insights must be changed; or the centre must acquire new skills; or the portfolio should be confined to heartland businesses.

2. Define how the centre is going to add value

There are five levers that corporate centres can use to create value:

- build

- develop

- leverage

- link

- stretch.

Select just *one, or at most two,* of these and concentrate on building up the corporate skill at applying this lever or levers.

3. Focus on heartland businesses

The portfolio should contain *only* heartland businesses: those where the value-creation insights can be applied by the centre using one of the five levers. For most corporations this will require disposing or spinning off many, and perhaps a majority, of current businesses. No matter. Do it.

You can then expand into, or acquire, other appropriate heartland businesses. But he careful with acquisitions. Only acquire where you can be fully confident that you will add more value than you destroy, and more net value than is required by any acquisition premium. If in doubt, don't do it. And if your current track record of acquisitions is ever poor or patchy, don't compound the question by making new ones. Quit while you're behind.

Smart examples of strategy

The five levers the centre can use to add value[11]

1. *Build.* Build propositions imply that the centre makes the business substantially larger and better positioned, often moving into new markets. The build proposition should be related to one or more value creation insights. For example:
   - consolidation of a fragmented industry, if there are potential economies of scale, network effects (where the larger player has higher utilization of assets), or where a brand premium can be obtained by the largest and most popular player;
   - internationalization, where there is an opportunity to take a winning formula and exploit it internationally, and/or to gain international economies of scale by making national segments into international ones;
   - convergence of technologies, as with NEC's long-established intention to merge telecom and computer industries (although whether this is true value creation insight or a delusion is open to question).
2. *Develop.* Develop is similar to Build, except it involves a direct injection of expertise into developing businesses (most Build propositions involve acquisitions and/or strategic alliances). Technology-based expansion strategies such as those of Canon (see next box) are Develop propositions: a new project is supported from central resources or in one or more existing divisions, and, as projects develop, they are formed into semi-businesses and potentially into new business units. Most core competency-based strategies are Develop propositions.
3. *Leverage.* Leveraging corporate assets or skills – such as brands, licences, patents, know-how or relationships – is a tricky business, but can sometimes be very successful. The Virgin brand and the Richard Branson phenomenon are clearly leveraged to great effect across all the Virgin businesses, clearly adding more value than they subtract.
4. *Link.* Link propositions are the use of cross-business synergies, sponsored or encouraged by the centre. As we have seen, there must be good reasons why the businesses themselves, as self-interested entities, are blocked from realizing synergies themselves; often, synergy is a mirage. Still, there are examples of successful link propositions: in financial ser-

vices, where a service network or distribution channel can sell many products; in industries where purchasing power is key and can be pooled between different business units; through sharing of know-how, as with Unilever's consumer marketing expertise.

5. *Stretch*. Stretch is an interesting proposition. Here the centre knows what type of performance can be obtained from an industry and ensures that all businesses stretch to meet this level. ABB and Emerson (see boxes) add value through Stretch propositions; in Emerson's case, businesses that used to make 5–10 per cent return on sales are stretched to reach 15 per cent. The Stretch proposition is often used in conjunction with heavy acquisition activity (and hence sometimes an explicit Build proposition) based around finding businesses that fit the Stretch profile. It is interesting that most successful venture capital investments are Stretch propositions.

4. Decide whether to restructure or breakup

You now need to work out an appropriate organizational structure and decide how to run the group. You have three possible choices:

(a) retain a conventional structure, probably similar to the one you have now, but with increased focus.

You should only select this option if it absolutely clear to you and all your key colleagues, including those in the businesses, that the new corporate strategy is attractive and will work. The value-creation insights, distinctive parenting characteristics, and heartland businesses must all be convincing in their own right and must all fit together. There must be clear evidence that the centre is in the unusual position of adding more value than it subtracts. And confidence in the new corporate strategy needs to exist not just at the centre, but in all the operating businesses.

Smart examples
of corporate
strategy

CANON[12]

Value-creation insights	Different product businesses like cameras, business machines, and specialist optical products can share the same technology base. It is therefore possible to make better products if one group can manage to share and cross-fertilize similar technological and market skills across different product areas.
	An inspiring corporate vision can help each business stretch for growth beyond the confines of each business
Distinctive parenting characteristics	Ability to stimulate cross-fertilization: • across technologies and markets • between technical and marketing experts High commitment to core technologies Ability to use company vision to stretch executives
Heartland businesses	Use of three core technologies: precision mechanics, fine optics, and micro-electronics Products confined to cameras, business machines and specialist optical products Products capable of being sold world-wide and through many different channels

A very sensible step, therefore, once you've devised your corporate strategy, is to take it to each of the businesses. Seek endorsement of the strategy. Conduct a secret ballot of the team in each business, where the executives can vote to endorse or reject the corporate strategy.

If the team in any business rejects the strategy, it won't work for them. You then have the choice of changing the strategy, or deciding that the business is not part of the heartland and therefore selling it or spinning it off. If there was a strong majority in favor of the strategy in all the other businesses, you'll probably decide the latter. But if there was only a bare majority in each of the other businesses endorsing the strategy, you should probably revisit and refine the strategy, or opt for *(b)* or *(c)* below.

If you do have a good strategy and opt for *(a)*, ensure that the centre can add value in its chosen way, but otherwise use an extremely light touch in dealing with the businesses.

Remember the hidden potential to destroy value every time you intervene. Delegate as far as you possibly can all decisions, including investments (but excluding acquisitions), down to the operating businesses.

EMERSON[13]

Value-creation insights	Sound businesses making 5–10% return on sales in the industries known by the Emerson central team can make 15% return on sales if the business unit strategies are tightened and manufacturing costs reduced, in accordance with the tried and tested Emerson formula
Distinctive parenting characteristics	Ability to run a detailed business unit strategy process to raise profitability Corporate Best Cost Producer (BCP) program Ability to stretch executives to achieve the 15% ROS target or better Skill in acquiring businesses that fit the profile
Heartland businesses	Manufacture of mid-tech electrical, electromechanical or electronic products for industrial customers

Smart examples of corporate strategy

Behave like a venture capitalist: if the business makes its numbers, don't interfere. If it doesn't, warn. If warning doesn't work, change the CEO.

(b) decide to breakup the corporation into two or more new ones.

The new corporations could either be SBCs or MBCs. If they are SBCs they do not need a corporate strategy. If they are MBCs, they do, so you will need to redefine the corporate strategy and test it as suggested in (a) above.

(c) there is a third choice: to decide to put the centre's ability to add value to the test of the market. This is a new option, actually combining (a) and (b), which I believe is totally original. Under my proposal (c), you would breakup the corporation into a number of SBCs, but also incorporate the centre as a separate corporation providing value added to the new SBCs.

The old 'group' would therefore continue to exist, but within a number of new, totally independent corporations. The old centre, now incorporated into a new corporation, would contract with the new SBCs to provide its corporate strategy services in exchange for a royalty or a share of profits. The contract would run for a defined period (say, five years) and then be renewable and renegotiable on both sides. The contract would also state whether or not the centre could offer its services to other SBCs outside the erstwhile group.

If the centre did not deliver value, the contract would be terminated. On the other hand, if the centre added a great deal of value, it might be able to negotiate more favorable terms, and by mutual agreement extend its services to other SBCs that did not compete directly with the original client SBCs.

How would it work? Let's assume that Richard Branson's Virgin group decides to spin off all its operating businesses and incorporate the centre as a separate business. The centre (renamed Virgin Central Inc) might retain the right to the Virgin brand and would contract to provide its other value-added services, such as the use of Richard Branson in 'events' and advertising.

Virgin Atlantic Airways, Virgin Cola, Virgin Railways, Virgin Lightships, and possibly other Virgin Airways (e.g. Virgin European Airways) and any other Virgin businesses would be set up as independent SBCs. These would then contract with Virgin Central for its services, probably on a royalty basis, for five years. At the end of the five years, each side would decide whether to renew the contract, and if so renegotiate the royalty.

The corporate strategy dilemma

The dilemma is that corporate strategy really can add value, and yet the structure within which corporate strategists must currently operate, the MBC structure, necessarily and inevitably destroys value.

Am I saying that the MBC, even with a good corporate strategy, always subtracts net value? No, not at all. The MBC may be a better solution economically than to split it up into separate SBCs and lose the value added by the centre.

What do I mean then, when I say that the MBC structure necessarily destroys value? What I mean is that, aside from the positive things added by the group and the centre, the structure of the MBC will destroy value in the ways documented earlier. Worse decisions are likely to be made by the MBC than by independent SBCs. Performance within the MBC will be blunted by the insulation syndrome, the alienation syndrome, and by all the subtle market-information-denying, information-discarding, and information-ignoring mechanisms that thrive in large and complex corporate bodies.

The advantages brought by the centre are forms of economic value-added that are not intrinsically structural or power-related. They are expertise-related.

The disadvantages of the MBC are not expertise-related. They are related to power, structure, information processing, accountability, and motivation.

It follows that it should be possible to benefit from the expertise without the disadvantages of the MBC structure. We should be able to have our cake and eat it. We can overcome the structural problem without liquidating the expertise inherent in corporate strategy. All we need to do is to inject another market level, that of the independent corporate centre, into the equation. In place of a centralized structure we can create a series of decentralized, focused corporations bound together in a market relationship for mutual benefit.

If we do this, we are corporatizing corporate strategy and incorporating the centre. If the centre has value to add it need not fear the market mechanism.

And the centre *does* have value to add. If this were not so, we would not have the problem of successful MBCs. Nor would we have successful venture capital companies.

For, in truth, my proposal is not as revolutionary as it sounds. Private equity firms provide the model for the value-adding but independent centre. Venture capitalists add value to the businesses they own in all the ways that centres do, with the sole exception of the linkage benefits. Yet the venture capital investee businesses are nearly always SBCs, independent, focused corporations, legally separate and able to take their own decisions. The most successful venture capital firms, like Bain Capital, have their own proprietary value creation insights, their distinctive parenting characteristics, and their heartland businesses. If venture capitalists can add value without the MBC structure, corporate centres can too.

Conclusion

Good corporate strategy is rare. It's hugely valuable. It's entirely feasible. It can be liberated from the structural constraints that too often turn value creation into value destruction. You now have the tools to construct an excellent corporate strategy, in collaboration with your businesses. Go forth and strategize!

Notes

1 1856–1950.

2 I have adapted my three questions from the two questions posed on page 5 of *Corporate-Level Strategy* by Michael Goold, Andrew Campbell and Marcus Alexander (John Wiley & Sons, New York, 1994). All quotations cited in this chapter as 'Goold, Campbell & Alexander' are from the book unless otherwise stated. It is the definitive work on corporate strategy and all smart strategists should read it. A great deal of the material in this chapter flows directly or indirectly from the book and from discussions with its three authors. I am grateful for their permission to use the extracts and ideas though I remain responsible for my own interpretation of them.

3 Director of the Ashridge Strategic Management Centre, and a leading authority on corporate strategy.

4 Commentary by Hamel in *The Ultimate Business Library* by Stuart Crainer, with Foreword and commentary by Gary Hamel (Capstone, Oxford, 1997); a very useful and witty guide to 50 key business books.

5 In their ground-breaking *Corporate-Level Strategy* (1994), based on ten years' research.

6 From *Breakup!* (Capstone, Oxford, 1997).

7 'Competitive Advantage to Corporate Strategy' in *Harvard Business Review*, May–June 1987, pages 43–59.

8 *Synergy* (Capstone, Oxford, 1998).

9　In 1912, when governor of New Jersey.

10　*Market Unbound* (John Wiley & Sons, New York, 1996).

11　See David Pettifer, *Corporate Centre Transformation* (Pricewaterhouse-Coopers, London, 1998).

12　Adapted from *Corporate-Level Strategy* by Goold, Campbell & Alexander.

13　Adapted from *Corporate-Level Strategy* by Goold, Campbell & Alexander.

7

The Big Picture

'The unseen hand of Adam Smith has been replaced by the visible hand of business bureaucracy.'

Adolf A. Berle Jr and Gardiner C. Means

Controversy warning!

Beware. This chapter presents a personal view of the trends in business and society. Though I have drawn very heavily on the ideas of Peter Drucker, Charles Handy, Tom Peters, Paul Krugman, Henry Ford, Joseph Schumpeter, James Burnham and F.A. Hayek, the cocktail I have create is very much mine. This a not a mainstream interpretation.

Does an essay on the big picture properly belongs in a book on strategy? Does the smart strategist need to read it? Good questions. Perhaps not. If you just want to be a good technical strategist, no. But things are happening in the world of business, and its relationship to society, about which anyone who works in business (and all responsible citizens) should be aware. If the strategist can't see the big picture, who will? And, believe me, there are powerful implications for your company and your career.

Make up your own mind about the *real* big picture.

Something is wrong with big business

Something is wrong with our large business corporations, and something is wrong with the market system in which they operate.

Today's typical large managerial corporation is not using society's resources efficiently or for the good of society. The current financial market system works disproportionately for the rich, favoring neither social justice nor economic enterprise. The smart strategist does not ignore these two issues. They will change the way that business is conducted in the future.

Enemy number one: the managerial corporation

The large multi-business managerial corporation's time has gone. It is neither efficient in terms of its own objectives, nor does it offer a decent working life to its employees, nor does it operate to society's benefit. The large

'If there is a single assumption that pervades conventional organizational theory it is that authority is the central, indispensable means of managerial control. This is not a consequence of man's inherent nature. It is a consequence rather of the nature of industrial organizations, of management philosophy, policy and practice.'

Douglas McGregor[3]

managerial corporation was a great and useful invention. Now it is needed no more. It will not, however, give up without a massive fight from the managers who have a vested interest in its continued existence. The managed corporation is helped in its fight for survival by the absence of better models or, in some cases, lack of awareness of them.

Why is the typical big business corporation not needed? Because there are better ways to run business – better for wealth creation, for people in business, and for society – without bureaucracy, without formal control systems, without much hierarchy, and even without *management* as an activity. Broadly speaking these are the methods of professionals, of the one-person business, of entrepreneurs, and of small business generally – and the ways of *free markets* rather than administered systems.

The forces at work in business and society – customer power, information power, investor power, global market power, simplicity power, and leader power – are making life difficult for large, and particularly large and diversified, managerial corporations.

Big business is losing market share to small business. Administered business is losing to entrepreneurial business.

'I think customer service is a really brilliant system designed to keep customers from ever getting service. My theory is that the most hated group in any large company is the customers. They don't know about company procedures or anything about what you do, which drives you crazy!

'At the same time, your bosses, who are idiots who don't have to talk to customers, tell you day in and day out that the most important person in the world is the customer.'

Dave Barry[4]

For the first time in history, large corporations are losing market share to smaller ones. In 1980, the Fortune 500 accounted for 60 per cent of American GDP; during the 1990s it had fallen to 40 per cent. And when the typical large corporation loses market share, it is not to another behemoth, but to smaller fry nibbling at the edges.

'Brain based companies have an ethereal character compared to yesterday's outfits ...

'Silicon Valley [is] arguably the most fertile 1,300 square miles in the world economy. It is also a carnival. I've had most of my assumptions about 'organization' ripped asunder as I've watched the Valley thrive ... it provides people with a heavy dose of liberation, and, God knows, it's disorganized.

'It's time to shed the old images [when] ... my eyes still turned mainly towards yesterday's big manufacturers.

'Now my gaze has shifted ... '

Tom Peters[5]

The advantage of size, like nostalgia, is not what it used to be. Complexity is slowing the responses of large corporations when speed is becoming the essence of competition. But most of all, large corporations waste huge resources on activities that are of little or no benefit (sometimes negative benefit) to customers. As markets become more effective, they clear in favor of the greater value provided by smaller and simpler business units. Disorganization has become more functional than organization. The Stalinist, integrated, diverse large organization, despite all its historical strengths and massive base of assets and know-how, cannot compete effectively in the new world.

Large corporations are having to learn to behave like smaller ones, whether through forced delayering and decimation of managers (the brutal and easy response, and the one most deployed to date), through splitting into two or more new corporations (a very intelligent and increasingly used response), or by changing their managerial structures and compensation systems (also an intelligent response, but one that goes against the grain and has been little used).

Smart quotes

'The basic problem afflicting large corporations can be described in one word: management. The solution requires three words: managing without management.

'Management is taking an increasing share of the wealth, it is adding complexity to decision-making processes and organization structure, and it is not devoting its time and effort to the marketplace.

'Today management, in aggregate, subtracts far more value than it adds.'

Richard Koch and Ian Godden[6]

In our quoted corporations, top managers typically focus on managing the capital markets – on managing earnings, which are meant to show a steady and predictable ascent – rather than looking after customers or the business itself. Perhaps this is only to be expected, since many large corporate CEOs are jumped-up accountants. But serving the stock market rather than the real market can lead to an air of increasing unreality in the executive suite. CEOs take refuge in mega-mergers or other 'events' that will increase earnings for a time but do nothing to help customers. If profits look like slipping, a standard response is to cut costs or put up prices, regardless of the implications for customer value or competitive position. It is small wonder that large corporations are prone to lose market share, even as their stock hits new highs on Wall Street. This is a game with a finite duration.

Apart from being parasites on both their past store of hidden wealth and the consumer, managerially-run corporations are also profoundly undemocratic, as almost every Dilbert strip exemplifies. Smaller businesses are

Smart quotes

'GrandMet, the UK multinational I worked for, had a quite astonishing variety of businesses ... but they all had one thing in common: the senior management of the different companies managed earnings as a priority, not the businesses or the markets …

'Pure cost-plus pricing is another sinner here – and the reason why America and Britain no longer have a consumer electronics industry …

'Customers do not give a flying fuck about your cost structure, or the math of your margin calculations, or your own view of your brand equity. They care about their value.'

Barry J. Gibbons[7]

In England, some years ago, there was a delightful academic named John A.T. Robinson, who became Bishop of Durham. He was most notable for questioning all the fundamentals of the Christian faith, including the Virgin Birth and the resurrection of Jesus Christ. His enemies claimed that he was an atheist. This the good Bishop denied, but it has to be said that his God was a very odd and ethereal one.

Charles Handy is to business thinking what John Robinson was to theology. Gentle, civilized, calm, reflective, scholarly, intellectual but with his feet planted firmly on the ground of our being, benevolent and whimsical, original and endearing, Charles Handy is definitely one of the smartest gurus for the very smart strategist. He is like a personal chaplain, asking you why you are doing things, what you'll get out of it, and how you'll take small or large steps to improve the world.

Gary Hamel said it well: 'Charles is one of the few management writers who can step entirely outside the world of management and then look back in. This outside-in perspective yields an uncompromising and unorthodox perspective which will discomfort and enlighten ... Where most business authors are intent on giving you the 'how', Professor Handy forces us to ask "why?" '

Charles Handy is the son of a southern Irish Protestant clergyman, got a First in Greats (classics) from Oxford, worked as an ex-pat for Shell in Malaysia and as an economist in London before becoming an academic at London Business School and MIT.

Since 1976, he has progressed from being a fairly conventional professor of managerial psychology and organizational behavior to becoming a pioneering thinker about work and society. The joy of Handy is to bask in his life-enhancing prose, so his books are more fun than any summary can indicate. His three most important ideas are probably the 'shamrock' organization, 'portfolio' of work, and the 'federal' structure for companies.

The shamrock organization is 'based around a core of essential executives and workers supported by outside contractors and part-time help', an idea explored in his 1989 book (and in my opinion still by far his best) *The Age of Unreason*, long before outsourcing became fashionable. Ahead of Tom Peters, Handy imagined that before long all successful companies would come to resemble professional service organizations like consultancies or advertising agencies. The core staff would be highly worked, highly rewarded, and be the heart of the firm; the 'help' would be fungible, replaceable and unimportant.

The core workers would comprise a meritocracy based on personal value added rather than hierarchy: 'smart people are not to be easily defined as workers or as managers but as individuals, as specialist, as professionals or executives, or as leader ... and they need to be obsessed with the pursuit of learning if they are going to keep up.'

Handy predicts that the full time job will become an anachronism. The total number of hours worked in a lifetime will halve, and the boundary between work and play will be blurred. Individuals will pursue not one job but a 'portfolio' of activities, splitting time between fee work, gift work, study, homework and leisure.

Handy also champions the 'federal' firm, in which the central function co-ordinates, influences and advises, but does not decide or dictate. The centre is concerned with long-term strategy and 'is at the middle of things', but the centre 'is not a polite word for the top or head office.' Most recently, Charles has provided his own visceral critique of capitalism in his 1997 work, *The Hungry Spirit*. I have an intuition, however, that the best of Handy is yet to come.

necessarily less undemocratic; the individual matters more. This is why most smart people prefer to work in smaller corporations, especially now the larger ones don't offer such superior security. And in a brain-centered economy this is another reason why most large corporations can't compete effectively.

'People who work for large corporations have no idea why they're being paid. We know in our souls we're not doing anything that needs to be done. We could fall down an elevator shaft and die, and the corporation probably wouldn't notice. We're not sure what we do, so we're afraid to say the wrong things. Whereas, back when people were shoemakers, they could say anything and people would still buy their shoes.'

Dave Barry

Yet the world is still full of inefficient, customer-unfriendly, market-un-friendly, employee-unfriendly, large managerial corporations – run by managers for managers. The times may be a-changing, but the managerial dinosaurs are very slow to die out. (How else can we explain the staggering success of Dilbert, which is rightly cynical about what happens in our corporations?) We need to give the dinosaurs a firm shove on their way.

Enemy number two: laissez-faire capitalism

Many agree that markets are better than managers. But, alas, the problem goes deeper than this. There is a problem with the current market system itself. *Not* with markets themselves. But with the way we have organized (and failed to organize) our markets.

Markets are neutral; they process the data they are given; and they are inherently biased towards those who have the most purchasing power. The problem with society today is that there is too big a gap between those who are included in the market system as its beneficiaries and those who are not. In the United States, most citizens are included but there is a

'The doctrine of laissez-faire capitalism holds that the common good is best served by the uninhibited pursuit of self-interest. Unless it is tempered by the recognition of a common interest that ought to take precedence over particular interests, our present system is liable to break down ...

'Because communism and even socialism have been thoroughly discredited, I consider the threat [to the open society] from the *laissez-faire* side more potent today ... we fail to recognize the need to sustain the values and institutions of an open society ...

'Wealth does accumulate in the hands of its owners, and if there is no mechanism for its redistribution, the inequities become intolerable. 'Money is like muck, not good except it be spread.' Francis Bacon was a profound economist.'

George Soros[8]

significant minority, about a fifth of the population, who are effectively outside the market system. In the developed countries of Europe this minority rises to around a third, and in poorer countries it is only a lucky minority who benefit from the market system.

The corporate system is dishing out increasingly skewed returns. Wealth is going to the owners of our corporations, the owners of equities, and these are not a representative sample of society. In the past 20 years, corporate America has grown its earnings at about ten per cent per annum, despite annual GNP growth only being around 3 per cent. Share prices have, in turn, grown much faster than corporate earnings. This amounts to a massive redistribution of wealth towards the wealthy and the comfortably off, at the expense of the bottom third of society.

Peter Drucker is, quite simply, the world's best writer on business, and has been since his first book was published in 1939. Drucker is the most fertile, most original, most prolific, and most far-sighted of all the gurus. Now, surely at the end of his life, his work is as sharp and provocative as ever. He has as good a claim to be one of the benevolent makers of the twentieth century as John Maynard Keynes, George Orwell, or any other writer, period.

Born into an upper-middle class Austrian family – his father was chief economist in the Austrian civil service – Drucker moved to England in the late 1920s, working as a clerk with a quill pen at a Bradford wool exporters and as a journalist and economist, before emigrating to America in 1937. In 1942 he became a consultant to General Motors, and soon after a professional writer.

Drucker's initial lodestar was the belief that management and the large industrial corporation had become the central profession and institution respectively in society. This was not an original belief, nor did it prove wholly correct. The early Drucker followed in the footsteps of such brilliant managerialists as Adolf Berle and Gardiner Means, and James Burnham, men whose faith in the power of management verged at times on the semi-fascist.

No matter. Drucker's belief in the power of rational management and organizing for results always went beyond the merely technocratic. He held that managers and organizations had responsibilities to customers and society that transcended purely financial obligations. This belief, again, was not original, but Drucker did more than anyone else to ensure that American capitalism took account of obligations to employees and customers and that integrity, once conspicuous by its absence in business, eventually became a prerequisite.

Certainly his emphasis upon the customer was powerful and fresh. In 1954, in The Practice of Management, Drucker penned the immortal words:

'There is only one valid definition of business purpose: to create a customer. Markets are not created by God, nature or economic forces, but by businessmen ... only when the action of businessmen makes it an effective demand is there a customer, a market.'

If Drucker did not start by being original, he has since notched up a string of 'firsts': first 'to see that the purpose of business lies outside itself', the first to see the decision process as central, the first to see that structure has to follow strategy, the first to champion management by objectives, the first to advocate decentralization, the first to invent the 'knowledge worker', the first to predict that state enterprises would fail and to advocate the 'reprivatization' of all institutions in society, including non-business organizations like universities; the first to see the significance of the information age and the transformation of capitalism; the first to insist that governments should govern but not 'do'; and one of the first to see that management and managers are passé, and that large corporations are (contrary to the dreams of his youth) more the problem than the solution.

A great innings, a great score, and an impossible act to follow.

Smart quotes

'Consider the free world's failure to extend a helping hand after the collapse of communism. The system of robber capitalism that has taken hold in Russia is so iniquitous that people may well turn to a charismatic leader promising national revival at the cost of civil liberties ...

'An open society is not merely the absence of government intervention and oppression. It is a complicated, sophisticated structure, and deliberate effort is required to bring it into existence. Since it is more sophisticated than the system it replaces, a speedy transition requires outside assistance ...

'Our global open society lacks the institutions and mechanisms necessary for its preservation.'

George Soros

On an international scale the problem is even more worrying. The free market system has proved a fair-weather friend to developing nations. The terms of trade, availability and price of capital, and exchange rates have all turned against the poorer countries.

Not only that. Corporations have increasingly begun *externalizing their risks*. The very high real returns to capital that have been increasingly characteristic of the past 30 years have not been matched by increasing risk, which alone is the social justification for high returns.

Au contraire! Managerial corporations have increasingly used their financial and political clout to lay off risk, transferring it to government, employees

'Capitalism has tried to insulate profit-making from commercial risk-taking ... capitalism has not got better at calculating or limiting its risks, but has simply transferred many of them to society in general and employees in particular. The process has resulted in a sharp reallocation of potential risk and rewards in favour of capital ...

'Without risk-taking there is very little social or political justification for profit-making ...

'The primary target of both cost-cutters and cost-shifters has been traditional employees. They have been casualised, contracted out, made part-time, temporary or partly-seasonal – flexible, in the catch-all weasel word of the 1990s ...

'In the process of making labour markets more flexible, the global economy has shifted the fulcrum between decision-making and risk-taking; employees are effectively being made to carry significantly more business risk and yet may not benefit from profits ... from having taken those risks.'

Bob Mills[9]

Bob Waterman was the co-author with Tom Peters of the mega-selling *In Search of Excellence*, but has since ploughed his own fascinating furrow. Previously a McKinsey veteran, working in Japan, Australia, Europe as well as his native California, he works part time in his consulting group, as a non-executive director of small companies, and 'when not disguised as a businessman, he paints and sells watercolors and oils'.

Laconic, laid-back and lateral-thinking, Waterman is now concerned with how companies renew themselves and how project teams – the 'adhocracy' replacing bureaucracy – can change the texture of organizations. He does not underestimate the difficulty: 'we are still living in a world created by Taylor [F.W. Taylor (1856–1917), one of the first management consultants and gurus, and the advocate of 'scientific management']: the specialization of work, mechanising things, dividing up work into functions.'

In his 1994 book, *What America Does Right* (published outside the US without the flag waving as *The Frontiers of Excellence*), Waterman looks at ten successful firms that 'put people first', including Federal Express, Levi Strauss, Rubbermaid and Merck. The people who are to be put first are employees and customers:

'Putting control further down the line [beyond making employees self-directed], even in the hands of the customer, is quite possibly the most radical departure from past management practice. It's also the most important.'

'Getting the customer to want you to succeed seems like a simple idea. It's not, but is at the heart of what we ought to mean by strategy.'

The book is notable for publicizing two discoveries. One was that American productivity was far ahead of its rivals: 25% ahead of Germany, 39% of Britain, and 64% ahead of Japan. One reason was very low Japanese productivity in service industries.

The other surprise was that a 30-year study of 15 companies that put people first showed that they had outperformed the Dow Jones index by 7.6 times!

He quotes a Johnson & Johnson executive, 'I have long harboured the belief that the most successful corporations – the ones that have delivered outstanding results over a long period of time – were driven by a simple moral imperative – serving the public in the broadest possible sense better than their competitors.'

and society at large. What is the delayering and downsizing carnage, but a massive transfer of risk from corporations to governments and employees? There used to be an implicit contract between the large corporation and its employees, which included job security. No more. Who pays the cost? Employees who lose their highly paid jobs, and governments who pay extra social security.

Small-business people still take real risks that may end in bankruptcy; the potential to make a fortune is balanced by the entrepreneur's risk of losing all her assets. I can't remember the last time I saw a large corporation and its top managers take real and personal risks, either for themselves or their shareholders, except through gross incompetence.

Twenty-First Century Solutions

What can be done?

1. *We should encourage the growth of small corporations.* Of course, they *are* growing, but we can lean further on this open door. The smart strategist might decide to do her bit, and join a smaller firm! But local and national government should encourage smaller corporations, as many are doing, with lower tax rates and exemptions from red tape.

2. *Investors and honest executives can decide to break up multi-business corporations, and establish the Single Business Corporation (SBC) as the preferred model for the next century.* Investors, executives, ordinary employees, customers, and society as a whole would all benefit enormously.

3. *We must reform the large managerialist corporations.* The owners – especially the large pension funds and insurance companies – should lead this process. They should insist that their investees either break up their companies or break down their managerial structures. Reform would include: the abolition of telephone number compensation for the top dogs; curbing stock options; dismantling of hierarchies; greater transparency of financial reporting; and firing executives who manage earnings rather than serve customers.

4. *Governments should withdraw the privilege of limited liability from the owners of large companies.* The Joint Stocks Acts in Britain and America in the first half of the nineteenth century gave a tremendous boost to industrialization. But now the field has been tilted too far in favor of owners and managers.

Smart quotes

'To build achieving organizations, you must replace power with responsibility'

Peter Drucker

The most important change in industrial organization in the first half of the twentieth century was the separation of ownership from control: the move from family owner-managers to professional managers with little ownership stake. The managers suffer too little penalty from irresponsible actions, since they can't lose what they don't own. Someone has to take responsibility, and it can only be the owners. Most investment institutions have behaved like absentee landlords, managing their bits of paper but rarely visiting their property.

'In the end, in bankruptcy, the effect of limited liability is to transfer some of the risks of investing in a business from its shareholders, who stood to make any profits along the way, to a company's creditors, who did not. From this perspective, it is trade creditors, lenders, employees and society as a whole (represented by the taxman), not shareholders, who finally underwrite business failure.'

Bob Mills

If owners did not enjoy limited liability, they would be bound to take more interest in their corporations. Managers' wings would be appropriately clipped.

It would be fair to exempt small business (and possibly all unquoted corporations) from this move. Unlimited liability for the entrepreneur would discourage start-ups and lead to risk-averse behavior, which would not be in society's interest. The same consideration does not apply to large corporations.

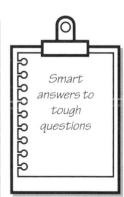
Q: Isn't it against the principles of the free market, which has created enormous wealth for the world, to place restrictions on large corporations and to deny them a level playing field?
A: Free markets do indeed create stupendous wealth.
   But large corporations hog resources within their walls and allocate the resources according to administrative fiat rather than market processes. Large corporations are the last bastions of socialist, centrally-planned, top-down resource allocation. Large corporations tend to waste society's resources, and society is entitled to reclaim those resources for truly free markets.

Smart
examples of
strategy

The democratic corporation

'Democracy has not yet made much headway into the corporation. The most successful institution of our society, some would say the dominant institution, the most powerful institution – this remains largely impervious to democracy. In a democratic world, the corporation is the last redoubt of hierarchy …

'The Democratic Corporation (DC) would be a firm where the shareholders and board of directors had agreed to let the employees vote, every few years, for the top management …

'Imagine this. Every four years the top management team of DCs formally announce, in July, their resignation, to take effect at the end of the year. The resignation triggers the election process, the start of the democratic campaign.

'Resources are then made available to qualifying groups of executives (and, if the rules allow, outside buy-in teams) who run for office. They present their manifestos – their strategies, their target markets, their internal policies, their ways of executing their designs. The manifestos are presented to the full body of employees in a series of campaign meetings, in leaflets, in videos, in more creative media. At the end of August, a vote is taken and one team emerges victorious. The team leader becomes the CEO and has a four year term to implement the vision.'

Richard Koch[10]

5. *Create a new class of company, the Democratic Corporation.* The Democratic Corporation is one in which the owners allow employees to elect the top management, subject only to shareholder veto.

6. Institute another new company type, the Capitalist Employee Collective.

The capitalist employee collective

'The Capitalist Employee Collective (CEC) is a new class of company, with two distinctive characteristics. All employees (after a qualifying period) are shareholders. And under certain conditions, the employees can, over time, come to own between them one quarter of the total share capital.

'All employees who pass their probationary period are granted a certain number of shares in the company, as a sort of delayed signing-on bonus or golden hello ...

'This would be just for starters. Employees would be entitled to receive more shares each year, but only if the company was performing very well. Individual firms would set their own criteria ... but one scheme might be that earnings per share would have to grow by at least 20 per cent for at least five years. If so, employees would receive extra shares constituting a given proportion of the surplus value over the 20 per cent earnings per share hurdle.

'For example, one firm might decide to allocate a flat rate of a quarter of the surplus value to employees in the form of shares. Thus, if earnings per share rose by 30 per cent, the initial shareholders would receive all of the first 20 per cent of the benefit, but only three quarters of the rest; their earnings per share would thus advance by 27.5 per cent, the other 2.5 per cent being allocated in new shares to employees ...'

Richard Koch

7. *Rig markets towards greater social equality.* Non-market ways of redistributing wealth don't take, because permanent capital is not acquired. Those who have capital can benefit from the extraordinary returns from capital. When society is divided into one group that has spare capital, and another that doesn't, it is inevitable that the gap in wealth between the two groups widens over time. If we value social stability and inclusiveness, this is not a good idea!

The only answer is to give all citizens some spare capital. In *The Third Revolution*, I discuss how to do this, including ideas for *Capital Start* (earmarked funds to start a business) and *Popular Privatization* (selling state assets but giving the proceeds to citizens rather than the state).

8. *Use markets to remove social deprivation and unemployment.* Typically, solutions to social issues like housing, education, health care, and jobs have involved creating non-market mechanisms. They have generally proved poor value. But markets can be used for all of these issues. If we wanted to, we could even reduce unemployment to very low levels, simply by using market mechanisms.

9. *A new Marshall Aid program for the developing world.* The Marshall Plan of 1948–51 was the most successful and far sighted use of capitalist dollars in the history of the world, laying the foundations for the recovery of war-wasted Europe, and for the golden age of capitalism that the world has enjoyed since. My suggestion is that George Soros should be given the equivalent sum (whatever Marshall's $12,500 million of 1948 dollars is worth in today's dollars) and told to get on with it.

Smart quotes

- 'The oppressive atmosphere in most large companies resembles downtown Calcutta in summer.

- 'You cannot renew a company without revitalizing its people.

- 'Companies that succeed are driven by internal ambition.

- 'Stock price doesn't drive them. Ambition and values drive them.'

Sumantra Ghoshal[11]

The big picture and your company

If you buy into this big picture, imagine what it might mean for your
  corporation:

- *If it's a big corporation, watch out!* You probably need to restructure it
  into smaller units, to remove large swathes of hierarchy, and to revital-
  ize your people. This won't happen without a real shift in attitude, a
  new commitment to change. Even with the commitment, it will take
  many years.

- Any large corporation and its strategists should *pay extra attention to
  small, growing competitors*, even if the danger from them seems remote.

- *Any corporation that is managing its earnings rather than serving its
  customers had better reverse its priority.*

- *Any manager who is mainly concerned with internal processes and management rather than adding clear value to customers needs: a change of
  mindset and a change of role, or a change of employment!*

- *Any corporation that is in more than one main line of business needs to
  examine whether it should break into two or more Single Business Corporations.*

- *Companies should consider become Democratic Corporations and/or
  Capitalist Employee Collectives.*

- *Small corporations should not fight shy of taking on their bigger brethren. The former are favorites to win!*

SMART PEOPLE
TO HAVE ON
YOUR SIDE:

IVAN
ALEXANDER

Ivan Alexander, one of capitalism's sharpest observers, is also one of its most successful industrial exponents. A critic of the calibre of George Soros or Charles Handy, Ivan Alexander also has the unusual credit of a lifetime's experience working in and running very successful businesses in Singapore, Indonesia, California, New York, Dusseldorf and London.

Ivan Alexander's reputation as a writer is spreading rapidly, largely as a result of *The Civilized Market*,[12] one of the most important business books of the decade. Robert G. Monks, chairman of the Lens Corporation, distinguished Republican Party politician, and himself an author, comments:

'If you ever wondered what has happened to all of the guiding principles of individualism and democracy in this era of great corporations, *The Civilized Market* is a joy. Ivan Alexander tells a wonderful story and weaves together strands of tradition and practice that are pleasurable and startling.'

In many ways, Alexander is like Charles Handy: he thinks unconventionally, writes beautifully; and challenges the reader to enrich the world. Yet Ivan Alexander's message is more upbeat. 'There is an affinity,' he asserts, 'between humanism, the idea of progress, and the business outlook.' Corporations 'are capable of more than they have yet achieved.' 'Business and humanism are not far apart ... industry and business are by definition in the business of service ... it is a short step to seeing them as resources of commonwealth.'

Using a wealth of historical and philosophical concepts, Alexander shows some surprising things. Competition is at the root of society's unprecedented wealth, yet business people do not like competition; nor is competition intrinsic to business values or practice. 'Competition is operable partly because of habits of tolerance and partly because of the rules of engagement set by society over many centuries.'

He insists that business depends not only on the concept of private property but also that of tolerance: 'free enterprise and free trade are forms of conduct inseparable from a high degree of tolerance.' Laissez-faire, aggressive capitalism, heedless of its consequences, is bad not just for society but for business as well:

Not only would [capitalism] be unaccepted in this Darwinian mould; it would not even work in it. Fortunately, its jagged edges are blunted by competition, by the conventions and countervailing actions of democratic politicians and governments; above all, by its own disposition for considered advances, timely retreats, compromise, and – tolerance.

It follows that institutional advances to democratize and civilize business are not merely justified by society; they are also essential for the health and wealth of business itself. Alexander is hopeful, however, that reform of business will come from within – from a realization that 'civilized' behavior and a service mentality are the real destiny of organizations. It is difficult to read *The Civilized Market* and not come to share Ivan Alexander's vision.

Finale

The implications of the big picture don't stop there. They also extend to the smart strategist personally, to her career within the corporation. The final chapter provides personal and career personal, professional and career advice for the smart executive.

Notes

1 Fortune 500 issue of *Fortune*, April 20, 1992. Drucker meant that the age of the mega-corporation was over.

2 American social psychologist.

3 1906–64, American industrial psychologist; *The Human Side of Enterprise* (McGraw Hill, New York, 1960).

4 Miami-based humorist; *Fortune*, July 1, 1997.

5 *Liberation Management* (Alfred A. Knopf, New York, 1992), which is well worth consulting for its many examples of how anarchic and disorganized successful companies now need to be.

6 *Managing Without Management* (Nicholas Brealey, London, 1997).

7 This former head of Burger King has produced one of the most funny and honest accounts of corporate life that I have ever read. It should be on the smart strategist's shopping list, and is, I promise you sincerely, really titled *If You Want To Make God Really Laugh Show Him Your Business Plan* (Capstone, Oxford, 1998).

8 Billionaire financier and philanthropist; 'The Capitalist Threat', *Atlantic Monthly*, February 1997.

9 Australian economist; 'Calculated Risks', *The Australian Financial Review Magazine*, 1998.

10 *The Third Revolution* (Capstone, Oxford, 1998).

11 Brilliant Indian academic and consultant.

12 Capstone, Oxford, 1997.

8

Crescendo: the Strategist in the Corporation

'Never confuse movement with action.'

Ernest Hemingway[1]

Advice for the strategist

Now is the time to draw together the threads of smart strategy for the smart strategist – for anyone in the corporation concerned with strategy: the CEO, non-executive directors, other Board members, the line executives, staff specialists, and ordinary front-line workers.

The 19 habits of smart strategists

1.   Think differentiation. This is the root of all successful strategy

Keep conjuring up the image of Gause's two animals with limited food in his bell-jars. Those who were the same killed each other. Those that were different survived.

> **Smart things to say about strategy**
>
> It's not enough to be excellent. You've got to be different as well.

To be successful in business, you *must* differentiate. Your company, your business unit, the activities for which you are responsible – they must all be different from those of competitors.

Excellent operational efficiencyis not enough if others have it too. You will enjoy profitless excellence together.

(By the way, this is true not just of your corporation, but also of your career within it. Unless you're different from everyone else – in some important way – you'll remain interchangeable with career rivals. For you too, it is actually more important to be different than to be excellent.)

> **Smart quotes**
>
> 'A company surrenders tomorrow's business when it gets better without getting different.'
>
> *Gary Hamel*

All great strategists innovate. Industry dynamics are never optimal. There's always a better way of doing things, a better system for pleasing customers at the same time as giving your own firm an economic edge. Differentiation requires innovation. An ounce of innovation is worth a ton of heavy-duty analysis.

2. Know your key idea

Every firm, every business unit, and every leader must have a key idea
or business concept that differentiates the business and makes
it special.

Peter Drucker calls this the 'theory of the business.' This
should not be complicated. In fact, it should be as short
and simple as possible. But it must also be real, and it
must be different from others' theory of their firms.

3. Think leadership

Leadership in a closely defined market – a certain type of activity for a
homogeneous group of customers – is the best measure of the success and
value of a business. Leadership positions are better than non-leadership
positions. Period.

The smart strategist knows where she has leadership positions and where
she does not. Where she does, she is obsessed with keeping leadership and

---

Peter Drucker's theory of the business[2]

'These are the assumptions that shape any organization's behaviour, dictates its decisions about what to do and what not to do, and define what the
organization considers meaningful results. These assumptions are about
markets. They are about customers and competitors, their values and
behaviour. They are about technology and its dynamics, about a company's
strengths and weaknesses. These assumptions are about what a company
gets paid for. They are what I call a company's theory of the business.'

Smart quotes

---

if possible extending it further. Where she does not, she has made a conscious decision either to seek leadership or not to. If she has decided not to, the market concerned is of peripheral concern to her. The smart strategist concentrates her efforts on actual and potential leadership positions.

Being the leader means, by definition, that one important group of customers has voted us number one. They think we're better than their other choices, better than our competition. We need to know why, or else our leadership position is in jeopardy.

4. Think customers, and talk to them

The smart strategist knows he's there to serve customers. There ain't no other reason to be in business. Most people accept this intellectually. But how often do they talk to customers? The smart strategist spends at least a third of his time talking to customers. (This also means the smart strategist is a rare breed, which is good news. The competition to be a smart strategist is not intense.)

5. Think competitors, and talk to them

You need to know what your competitors are thinking. Competition is not a zero-sum game: you can win, and they can too. Encourage competitors to be different too. Manage competitive rivalry constructively. Collaborate where this is possible and legal. Industries where competitors are hostile to each other or where they never communicate nearly always have lower profitability than when the opposite is the case.

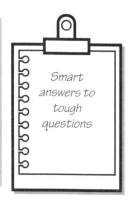

Collaboration should not remove the need for differentiation, but should sharpen its edge constructively, to the benefit of customers. For example, in the consulting business, sensible firms will often refer a client to the competitor whom they consider best for the job, either when the firm originally approached has no capacity or when the job is not quite in their power alley. In the private equity (venture capital) business, firms will often take positions in deals put together by their rivals. It is no accident that consulting and private equity tend to be extremely profitable.

6. Think economics

All successful business is based around having high return on capital. This, in turn, usually requires fat margins. This means that the gap between your prices and your costs (all costs) must be sustainably sizeable. This cannot be so unless you can give the customer something she really values at a cost significantly lower than your price, and also significantly lower than any competitor's cost. It is no use delighting the customer if you cannot do so at a decent margin: her delight, and your existence, will be short-lived.

All business success is based around micro-economics, that profit equals price minus cost times volume. Unless you have found a successful and distinctive way of running this formula, in a way that your competitors cannot do as favourably, or cannot do at all, you have no sustainable competitive advantage.

7. Think big

How can you change the rules of the game in your business?

How can you establish a better way of delivering what customers want at lower cost? The smart strategist will know that there's *always* a way, and won't give up until he's found it.

8. Think small

Specialization is the path to wealth. Segment your markets into small systems where you can innovate, dominate and enrich both the customer and your firm.

9. Focus

Find out what the best 20 per cent of your business is – the things you do best and most profitably – and do more of it. Worry about this 20 per cent and not the other 80 per cent.

At the heart of strategy is resource allocation. Progress requires taking resources from less profitable activities and redeploying them in more profitable ones. The biggest mistake that most business people make is to keep unproductive resources going. The essence of entrepreneurship is to identify the most productive activities and throw everything at them. This necessarily requires a tight focus.

Focus your own efforts too, on what you do best.

10. *Think value; manage value, not the numbers*

The smart strategist knows that business is a game of mutual value creation. The business creates value for the customer and the other way round.

In large and complex businesses, especially viewed from the executive suite, there is a strong tendency to think otherwise: to imagine that business is a game of manipulating profit numbers, so that they always point upward.

The smart strategist knows that this is a slippery slope. Once you start managing the numbers and not value creation in the business, you have gone astray and there is no easy way back to the paths of righteousness. Resist the temptation. If you see colleagues succumbing, point out their error. If they ignore you, take your talents somewhere else, where you can play the business game honestly.

11. *Experiment. Use the market*

The smart strategist experiments. It's often cheaper than analysis and market research, and always much more

'The 80/20 Principle asserts that a minority of causes, inputs, or effort usually leaders to a majority of the results, outputs, or rewards. Taken literally, for example, 80 per cent of what you achieve in your job comes from 20 per cent of the time spent. Thus for all practical purposes, four fifths of the effort – a dominant part of it – is largely irrelevant.'

Richard Koch[10]

reliable! The market will tell you when you've got it right. Find low-risk and inexpensive ways to experiment.

The most successful people in any walk of life are endlessly curious, endlessly experimenting. If you do the same thing time and again, how can you possibly learn anything?

People often tell you that experimentation is 'too risky'. Ask them if they ever calculate the risk of doing nothing.

12. Cut your losses early

When the market has proclaimed a move dumb, the smart strategist takes heed. Loyalty to colleagues, reluctance to admit a mistake, belief that perseverance is a virtue, laziness, groundless optimism, and a wish not to rock the boat – all these conspire to make organizations ignore their mistakes. If the business makes a loss this year, perhaps it may break even next ... And when next year comes, and the business is making an even greater loss, well, perhaps this, that or the other will make all the difference. Perhaps. But probably not.

Smart quotes

'If people never did silly things, nothing intelligent would ever get done.'

Ludwig Wittgenstein[12]

'The trouble is, if you don't risk anything, you risk even more'

Erica Jong[13]

The smart strategist listens to the market. Investing in failure is not one of her vices. It is a tricky business, combining creativity and imagination on the one hand with scepticism on the other. All great strategists can perform this balancing act.

> Smart things to say about strategy
>
> Don't buck the market.

13. Look for unexpected successes

When something succeeds without warning, when sales and profits of a small business roar ahead of budget, when customers can't get enough of something you didn't expect them to like much, then ride the wave for all it is worth. As Shakespeare wrote, there is a tide in the affairs of man ...

One of the most useful things a strategist can do is to find in the bowels of the corporation a little business that no-one is paying attention to, but

> Smart things to say about strategy

There's much greater value in making a successful business even more successful than in taking an unsuccessful business and making it so-so. It's also normally a lot easier.

which is doing really well. Shift money and talent its way. Roll it out for all it's worth, before competitors notice and work out the formula.

14. Build on strengths; don't correct weaknesses

When you have to be better than pesky competitors, only strengths will do. It's one of the ironies of organizational life that the best talent is usually deployed doing the most difficult jobs, solving the most intractable problems. This is daft. The best people should be doing the easiest jobs, consolidating success. They'll do it better than anyone else, and the payoff will be much greater.

This goes for your own career too. Avoid the difficult challenges. Go for the successes. And only do things that play to your own strengths.

15. Develop strategy in action

The smart strategist follows Henry Mintzberg's advice, and crafts strategy as she goes along, mixing action, experimentation, and thought. Strategy is not so much a plan as a process. Market feedback and a realization that the organization either can or can't hack it ahead of the best competition are essential ingredients of strategy. And true commitment can only be expressed in action.

16. Have a mental map of where you're going

Maps have become unfashionable amongst those who advise us to craft strategy. I don't know about you, but I hate driving in an unfamiliar re-

'People act in order to think.'

Karl Weick[16]

'Think like a man of action, act like a man of thought.'

Henri Louis Bergson[17]

Smart quotes

The Hungarian soldiers lost in the Alps: a story of maps, ignorance and confidence

This is a true story, told by Karl Weick.

A Hungarian troop of soldiers got lost in the Alps during manoeuvres. It snowed for two days, they were frozen and hungry, and they lost the will to live. Then a miracle intervened. Suddenly one of the chaps found a map in his pocket. The detachment followed the map, marching confidently out of the mountains to safety.

Happily, it was only when back at camp that they discovered the map was of the Pyrenees. Ignorance and confidence are a potent duo.

Smart examples of strategy

---

gion without a map. Even a bad map is better than none at all. You can correct a bad map. Having no map makes us victims of pure chance.

17. *Reflect and think, even as you act*

Movement is not intelligent action. Only action designed to get you somewhere is worthwhile. Think while you act. If this is impossible, prefer thought to action.

18. Take responsibility, have a Cause, be a leader

Leadership requires that you try to improve on the status quo. To be effective in your quest for change, you need to define it succinctly and attract followers to the Cause.

The strategist *must* be a leader, just as a leader must be a strategist. Even if in a humble organizational role, there is nothing stopping the smart strategist asserting his leadership. A strategist without a Cause, or without followers, is dead in the water.

> Smart examples of strategy

The idea of a cause

'To lead well, you must excite.

'Good leaders turn people on. A tiny minority of leaders do this by inspiring leadership: by charisma, force of personality, unusual charm or compelling presence. You either have this or you don't, and most of us don't. If leadership required charisma, the world would be a much poorer place.

'It doesn't require exceptional interpersonal skill to excite people. It requires a Cause: something that gets people to want change to happen.

'*Freedom* is a great Cause. *Eliminate starvation* is a great Cause. *Build a cathedral* is a great Cause. A Cause is attractive to those you which to influence ...

'You cannot become an effective leader without a Cause ... A Cause mobilises. A Cause attracts.'

Richard Koch[18]

Define *your* Cause. It could, for example, be decentralization. It could be the break-up (de-merger, unbundling, spinoff) of the corporation into two or more new independent entities. It could be the opposite: achieving a merger with another firm. It could be a strategic alliance. It could be higher profitability based on focus. It could be attaining leadership in one particular business. It could be a transformation in levels of service or quality. It could be something else entirely. But the smart strategist will always have a Cause, and, when it is reached, will select another one.

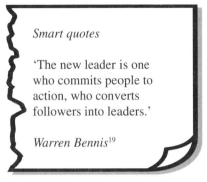

19. Finally, encourage all executives to become leaders

There are two particularly harmful myths about business and leadership. One is that each unit should have only one leader. The other is that a democratic or open business culture does not need leaders. Both beliefs are 100% wrong. Progress requires change; change requires leaders; and there is no danger of having too much leadership. Organizations suffer a perpetual deficit of leadership. If this were not true, the organization would be providing a perfect service, competition would be unnecessary, and we would irrevocably have reached the end of history. Improvement requires leadership. There can never be too much improvement. There can never be too much leadership. We must all be leaders and we must all be followers.

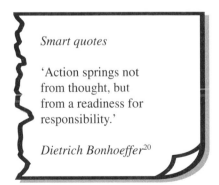

These nineteen habits of smart strategists apply whenever you are working, and in whatever role. In addition, I'd like to suggest a few *daily* habits, and then a few habits specifically geared to different jobs within the corporation.

The daily habits of the smart strategist

Spend some time each day thinking!

Activity does drive out thought, and some quiet thought each day is essential. *What* are you trying to achieve, *who* do you need to persuade, *what information* do you need that you don't have, and *what actions* are most likely to conduce toward your success?

I try to persuade executives not to schedule meetings before 10 a.m., so that there is time for some thought each day. If she can't do this, the smart strategist will block out some time and place each day where she can't be disturbed (and she will not answer the phone).

Another excellent habit is to spend an hour each day exercising, and to plan this into your schedule. When you exercise, you can also think.

Refill the creative hopper

Being a good strategist requires creativity. Creativity requires feeding. Spend some time each day absorbing the nutrients of creativity – stimulating conversation, visual arts, music, natural beauty, watching a film or play, reading, writing.

> *Smart quotes about strategy*
>
> 'What is this life, if full of care,
> We have no time to stand and stare?'
>
> *W. H. Davies*[21]

These are much better uses of time than reading the e-mails, listening to the voicemails, writing or reading memos and faxes, and all the other trivial rounds of daily office life. If there's anything you really need to know, someone will tell you – or you can ask them, face to face.

Overwork is an endemic disease of successful business people and it corrodes creativity. The smart strategist must have time to ponder. It's easy to steal this time from the useless time sink of trivial corporate activity.

Don't waste time!

Organizations are conspiracies to waste as much time of as many people as possible; and the larger and more complex the organization, the more time will be wasted. Well, this is not inevitable. Opt out. Let other people waste each other's time, not yours. A smart way of not wasting time is simply not to be there.

Don't do things that you wouldn't do if you were in business on your own account.

> *Smart things to say about strategy*
>
> We can't just sit around doing nothing; people will think we're from Head Office.

Prepare for meetings and keep them short

The smart strategist will always work out what it is that she wants from meetings. If the answer is 'nothing', she won't go. If it's something, she'll try to get to that as quickly as possible, and then leave.

If a meeting attains its purpose in 15 minutes, don't be afraid to suggest that it was a great meeting with no need to continue. This can make quite an impression.

Most people just turn up for meetings. The smart strategist prepares for them carefully. This doesn't mean spending a lot of time or preparing copious paperwork. It does mean thinking. Prepare questions that need answering, and be ready to summarize the issues as you see them.

Talk to customers today or tomorrow

If you didn't talk to any customers (or potential customers) yesterday, do so today. If you aren't talking to any customers today, ensure you do so tomorrow. Make this an inflexible rule. If you can't keep it, find another job.

Special advice in developing strategy ...

... for the CEO

• Don't decide strategy too quickly, especially if you are new.

• Consult widely on what the strategy should be, what the firm is good at, where it has competitive advantage. Collect opinions at all levels.

• Pay particular attention to the views of your young people, the most junior people, and front line people who deal with customers day in and day out.

• Surround yourself with people who will disagree with you. This is more difficult than you might imagine.

• Don't decide anything to do with strategy until you have talked to customers and competitors, especially to customers (and people who aren't customers, but could be).

- Don't move faster than the organization can deal with. Don't leave your followers behind. Wait for them to lead you on. Then strike.

... for non-executive directors

- Attending board meetings and using your experience are not a sufficient basis for strategizing. Don't overestimate your knowledge of the company. If you really want to contribute to strategy, get out and talk to the troops and to customers.

- It is easier to spot that the company has a wrong strategy than it is to create the new strategy. But spotting that, and doing something about it, is an incredibly valuable role, and one that, nine times out of ten, only non-executive directors can fulfil.

... for line executives

- Never forget that strategy belongs to you. It's your business and it must be your strategy. Don't let anyone take it away from you. Take responsibility even when it is not clear that you have authority.

- Remember to break things down into competitive segments.

- Remember to establish, for each segment, whether or not you have competitive advantage.

- Focus your efforts, people and cash only on the segments where you have or can have competitive advantage.

- Always tell Head Office the truth. And if they tell you to do stupid things, emulate Admiral Nelson at the battle of Trafalgar: put the telescope to your blind eye.

- Always spend two days a week with customers.

... for staff specialists

- remember you are facilitator, not a member of the secret police

- even if you are from Head Office, take a populist, anti-Head Office stance. Encourage line executives to take responsibility for their strategy.

- develop trust. Be absolutely straight. Do not betray confidences.

- don't spend too long in the job. Find an area where you can practise what you preach.

> *Smart things to say about strategy*
>
> 'Someone has to do something, and it's just incredibly pathetic that it has to be us.'
>
> Jerry Garcia[26]

Final Career Pointers for the Smart Strategist

Remember the big picture painted in the previous Chapter? Well, if you subscribe to it, there are certain career corollaries, to wit:

1. The future does not belong to large corporations. If you're in one, plan your escape. If you're not, don't get trapped in one.

2. Work in the best company in your industry. It's incredibly dumb to do anything else.

3. Specialize by industry as well as role. The day of the generalist is over.

4. Ensure that there's one thing that you can do better, and that you know more about, than anyone else around.

5. Be different from your peers, and ensure that you are perceived to be different.

6. When considering a career move, choose your new company with all the wiliness and care that you would apply to competitor analysis. From the shortlist of possible companies, choose the best one, the winning one, the one that is expanding, the most profitable, the one that pays the most, the one with the best reputation for cherishing and developing its people.

7. If at all possible, organize a leveraged/management buy out (LBO/ MBO). By taking absolute responsibility for your fate, you'll learn a tremendous amount. You might also just make a fortune.

8. Look out for areas of potential opportunity, while in your current job, for a new venture. When the time is right, start your own business. This is the greatest contribution you can make to the economy and society. Then you can really have fun crafting your own strategy.

Over to you

We're now at the end of the book and the beginning of your new or improved life as a smart strategist! I've done the easy part. But I trust that, in tackling the messy and unpredictable realities of business and life, you'll confidently craft strategy to create a richer world.

Two final smart quotes about strategy

'Take a chance! All life is a chance. The man who goes the furthest is generally the one who is willing to do and dare.'

Dale Carnegie[27]

'Just do it!'

Nike slogan[28]

Notes

1 1899–1961, American man of letters.

2 Managing in a Time of Great Change *(Butterworth-Heinemann, London, 1995)*.

3 Basil Fawlty, English hotelier, to his customers; from John Cleese's fab TV comedy, *Fawlty Towers*.

4 American humorist; *Fortune*, July 7, 1997.

5 1729–97, British political philosopher.

6 British economist and strategy guru.

7 1757–1827, British artist and poet.

8 Architect.

9 French economist and philosopher, who invented the word 'entrepreneur' around 1800.

10 *The 80/20 Principle*.

11 1809–82, English gentleman, anturalist and developer of the theory of evolution. Competition between species was key to Darwin's theories.

12 1889–1951, German philosopher.

13 1942– , feminist writer.

14 The world's most successful investor.

15 British entrepreneur and inventor during the Industrial Revolution.

16 American academician.

17 1859-1941, French philosopher.

18 *Moses on Leadership, Or, Why Everybody is a Leader* (Capstone, Oxford, 1999).

19 1925–, American social psychologist, futurologist and master of leadership studies.

20 1906–45, German theologian, who took responsibility for trying to kill Hitler.

21 1870–1940, British poet.

22 1900–1993, the man who taught the Japanese to make quality products.

23 Describing the views of Richard Pascale, a pathbreaking American author and academic, in *The Ultimate Business Library* (Capstone, Oxford, 1997).

24 1924–, British industrialist.

25 1919–90, founder of the eponymous magazine.

26 1942–95, leader of The Grateful Dead, American rock band.

27 1888–1955, best-selling American author and merchant of hope, and the second super-star of self-help (after British author, Samuel Smiles).

28 Many of the apparently 'general' quotations in this chapter that I have used to illustrate strategic themes are derived from Stuart Crainer's excellent anthology, *The Ultimate Book of Business Quotations* (Capstone, Oxford, 1997).

Index

lasers 135
LBO *see* leveraged buy out
leadership 203–4, 212
    segmentation 93, 95–8
Lennon, John 26
leveraged buy out (LBO) 151, 155, 219
limited liability 192–3
line executives 217–18
linkage initiatives/synergy 155–6
Lochridge, R.K., quote 101
Luchs, K.S., quote 58

McDonald's 128, 133
McGregor, Douglas, quote 179
management buy out (MBO) 155, 210
managerial corporations 178–82, 184–5
    reform of 192, 197
    and risk 189, 191
maps 210–11
market feedback 47, 210
market opportunities 55–6
market research 207–8
market share 85–6, 133
    smart answers 91
markets
    and social deprivation/unemployment 196
    and social equality 195–6
Marshall Aid program 196

Marx, Karl 64
MBC *see* Multi-Business Corporation
MBO *see* management buy out
Means, Gardiner C., quote 177
Microsoft 43, 73, 128
Mies van der Rohe, Ludwig, quote 207
Mills, Bob, quotes 189, 193
Mintzberg, Henry 40
    profile 48–9
    quotes 37, 38, 66
mission 67
    smart answers 66
Moltke, Graf von, quote 40
Monks, Robert G. 198
Moore, Geoffrey 44
Morita, Akita 90
Mulgan, Geoff, quote 134
Multi-Business Corporation (MBC) 143–5
    breakup of 192
    dilemma 171–3
    failure of 145–6
    and value-destruction 146–59

Napuk, Kerry, quote 2
NEC 59, 131–2
Netscape 43
niche market 71, 133
non-executive directors 217
Nordstrom department store 127

economics 205–6
encourage executives to
    become leaders 213
experiment 207–8
focus 206–7
have a Cause 212–13
know key idea 203
leadership 203–4, 212
look for unexpected successes
    209–10
mental map of where you are
    going 210–11
reflect/think as you act 211
responsibility 212
strengths/weaknesses 210
think big 206
think small 206
think value 207
strategy
  business unit versus corporate
      20–21
  case against 25–6
    advantage as illusory/tempo-
        rary 42–7
    instinct versus analysis 32–42
    long-range planning 26–8
    recognised or constructed 49–
        50
    ritual 28–32
  creators/users of 15–16, 18–20
  defined 1–7
  guide to 21–3

killer questions/smart answers
    10, 28, 36
planned/actual 4
quotes 107
as shambles 27
superior/different 5–7
versus operational effectiveness
    7–11
strategy consultant 16–19
synergy 155–6
  and enlightened self-interest
      paradox 156

Timex 61
Total Quality Management (TQM)
    8
Toys 'R' Us 137
trade-offs 9
truth possession/perversion paradox
    154–5

unbundlings see breakups

value creation 161–2, 169
  insights 163–4
Value Destruction theory
  and central staff services 156–7
  and executive influence 153–5
  explained 146–53
  and linkage initiatives/synergy
      155–6
  and portfolio development 157–9